Dulcelle!
Kiitti!

[signatures]

jimi

tenor

OMNIVERSE

contents

spaces

Foreword 11
Sökö, Helsinki, 1990 13

The Communist Party Dancehall, Kauklahti, Espoo, 1995 16
Sheffield, 1996 23
Helsinki, 1997 26
Paseo De Picasso, Barcelona, 1997 29
London, 1997 31
Lodz & Warzaw, 1999 32
Lary 7's Studio, New York, 2012 36
Jimi's Home Studio, 2022 40

people

Lary 7 46
Russell Haswell 48
Nicole Willis 52
The Soul Investigators 55
Tony Allen 56
Itetune 61
Kabukabu 64
Max Weissenfeldt 67
Petri »Pete« Toikkanen 69
Maurice Fulton 70
Jori Hulkkonen 73
Matti Knaapi 74

Actions

Crane Show, Urban Rock, Helsinki, 1988 79
Sähkö Tour, Glasgow, 1994 81
Tenorwear, Sala Apolo, 1997 82
Backdrop, Barcelona, 1998 86
Sónar Festival, Barcelona, 1998 89
Afterparty, Barcelona, 1998 91
Barbican Centre, London, 2000 92
Jimi Tenor And Rhythm Taxi, Berlin, 2004 97
World Expo, Shanghai, 2010 100
Sauna, Lahti, 2006 103
French Culture Centre, Nairobi, 2011 104

objects

Flute 109
Korg MS20 110
Sirkka The Drum Machine 115
Atari 520 123
Log-O-Phone 125
Zither 129
Photophone 131
Score For Night In Mogadishu Ave 135
Solo Gig Settings 136
Kimono 138

Art

Jimi By Thron Ullberg, New York City, 1992 143
Washington Heights Rooftop Portrait, New York City, 1992 147
Opening At Orensanz Foundation, New York City, 1993 148
Empire State Building Reflexion, New York City, 1993 152
Tiina Medusa, New York City, 1993 155
Wrestlers Grand St. Gym, Williamsburg, New York City, 1993 157
Z Factor, New York City, 1993–1994 158
Tacheles Exhibition, Berlin, 1994 173
Urinator, New York City, 1994 175
Midsummer Night Video, Lake Päijänne, 1998 179
Autobahn, Finland, 2011 183

outro

Coney Island, New York, 2010 188
Photo Credits 191

The story which I am about to unfold
is a personal quest in time
written in music and light
and some words on the side

There was no aim in my journey
I mainly followed the arrow of time
My lowly fight against entropy
was chaotic at times, you may find

I've seen the big cities
and I've lived in a few
but I'm a man of modest needs;
I prefer to do my albums at home
and take photos of the people near me

Perhaps I am more
like a painter of sounds,
my albums like those ready-mades;
I make a collage of some chords that I've found
and I glue it with a lick of guitar

I invite you to enjoy
the stories I've told
and the photos I've taken and found

This is my contribution
in the artform of books,
enough of ranting –
let's have a look!

Foreword

Jimi beamed into my life, seemingly from outta space in 1994. I knew nothing at all of his history and assumed the incredibly inspiring »Sähkömies« album I had discovered in my local record shop was his first, perfectly formed release. He was exactly what I needed at that point in time. I had been lost in a Techno wormhole for over half a decade. As it was becoming an increasingly conservative musical form I knew I needed to find a way out. Jimi was the shining light at the end of the tunnel that helped point in a different direction. That direction ended up being Optimo and a quarter of a century later I am still in thrall of the ›new‹ direction he helped me locate.

We live in a world where success is increasingly measured in numbers, followers and likes and is often just a short term burst of hype and then forgotten.

I'd argue that in the true measure of the word that Jimi has been fantastically successful. He has sustained a career in music for decades, on his own terms, making the music he wants to make, collaborating with some of the greatest, making fantastic album after album and entertaining countless audiences. No sell out. This is success! This is the magic formula. Jimi has found that pot of gold at the end of the rainbow.

We had Jimi come and play Glasgow so many times that I lost count. We would have endless discussions about booking someone for one of our parties and it would always come down to »but will they be as good as Jimi?«. The answer would invariably be »No«, so we'd invite him yet again. So it goes that he entertained a generation of Glaswegians. There are so many stories but as I have to keep this introduction brief I will just tell this favourite tale. It is New Year's Eve 1995 (or Hogmanay as we call it in Scotland, where it is a really, really big deal). We have a party at the 2000 capacity Barrowlands Ballroom. It is sold out. »Take Me Baby« has been the tune of the year and Jimi is due onstage as the bells strike midnight. Jimi has been having a few drinks backstage and has lost track of time, and lost his glasses. He has to be on stage NOW so I hurriedly usher him on. He walks to the front of the stage, without his glasses, and addresses the fervidly expectant audience. »Happy New Year Glasg…« but before he can finish the sentence he has fallen head first off the front of the (famously high) stage. It must have hurt like hell but Jimi doesn't miss a beat and carries on as if it was part of the show. The entire audience, now believing it was all planned, go next level nutsoid. To this day people come up to me and talk about that wild Jimi Tenor show where he dove head first off the stage. What a star!

It would be impossible to invent Jimi Tenor's life. If this book was fiction it would all seem a bit far fetched.

Electronic Space Jazz Afro Funk Cosmic Soul Soundtracks forever.

JD Twitch 27/01/22

Sökö, Helsinki, 1990

I once saw some strange photos taken with an Omega photo finish camera. The cool thing about a photo finish camera is that it keeps taking pictures of the same spot, but if you pan a little you get bizarre results. I guess there's a similar function in the panorama mode of a modern phone camera.

My friend Petri Anttonen made his own version in which a very narrow slit would move through the film area during the exposure. He used an electric motor to move the slit, which he'd fashioned from two carpet knives. I was so impressed with Petri's version that I decided to make my own crude version of this idea, so I created a small slit in front of the camera lens and moved the film manually, firing a flash after each tiny movement of the film. This could only work in a dark room.

When my camera was ready to use I asked my friend Sökö (who went on to make the »Midsummer Night« video) to be my model. I wanted him to be a bit like the Hindu god Shiva, and was very happy with the final result. We celebrated with champagne and then went out to a local club. For some reason these rich kids coming out of the club annoyed me while we stood in the queue and I hit one of them in the balls with my knee. I was totally shocked at what I'd done and started to apologise while the guy rolled around the floor in agony. Well, his friends beat me up pretty badly, knocking me to the ground and kicking me, and who could blame them? I have never done anything like that before or since. I'm not a violent person.

spaces

The Communist Party Dancehall, Kauklahti, Espoo, 1995

In 1996 we lost our apartment in Helsinki and needed a place to stay urgently. One of Tiina's best friends, Markku Arokanto, lived in a disused communist party dancehall in Espoo and said that we could have the old kitchen and one extra room for something like 50 € a month—almost nothing. The catch was that our bathroom was an outhouse and since there was no running water we had to use a wheelbarrow to get water from a public well about 1 kilometre away. Though the room was beautiful, the building was only designed to be used during the summer months and it was very difficult to heat by natural fire alone. We ended up living in an office on the other side of the building which was thankfully better constructed.

In the early 20th century the dancehall was swinging but by the time we lived there it was abandoned. The communist party had dismantled itself when the Soviet Union collapsed and people didn't actually know who owned the building anymore. Our neighbour told us that people used to come to the dances by rowboats and small sailing boats and there were still big iron mooring rings in the cliffs next to the outhouse. But the strange thing is that there is no sea anywhere near the place now. The nearest shore is about 2 kilometres away! During the ice age there was a very thick layer of ice in Finland, perhaps 2 to 3 kilometres thick, which pushed the ground down with its weight. Now that the ice has melted, the ground keeps rising, and during the last hundred years the Earth has risen so much that the shoreline is 2 kilometres away from the building.

The main hall had wonderful acoustics so I did a lot of recording there during the spring and summer, including the track »Tesla«. The idea of the song was to capture the mood when Nikola Tesla was living in the New Yorker Hotel towards the end of his life. Apparently he talked mostly to pigeons at that point with little human contact. I placed the vocal mic at a distance to get a room sound and recorded the song in one go; all the dub effects, vocals and solos in a single take! Although I did need about fifty attempts to get it right. I still had my Eko Rimini-organ for that song. I loved that organ. Too bad I drowned it in lake Päijänne making the »Midsummer Night« video.

At first we didn't have a phone, but once we got a landline Steve Beckett from Warp called me and said he would be interested in signing me. He'd seen me play in Vienna, where Mika Vainio put a leberkäse on top of my organ during the set. I guess my performance was just bizarre enough …

So eventually I got signed and thought I could use the surroundings of the communist party dancehall to create some special PR shots. I liked to combine glamour with primitive conditions and to make it perfect I didn't have to change anything at the house or in my wardrobe. Tiina was crazy about clothes so I could always find nice details for my outfits from her collection, and the communist party placards and flags we found in the attic were great props—I didn't care at all about the political message, but the look was just right.

Sheffield, 1996

In 1996 Warp invited me to Sheffield to record the *Intervision* LP. I was very excited to do an album in the UK because I thought it meant that I was for real or something. Then again, a lot of great albums have been made in Sheffield, so maybe there was good reason to be excited. The city reminded me of my hometown Lahti in a way—a place that until recently had been a very busy industrial town and was now trying to find a way to survive in the modern global economy. The good thing about both places is that there aren't that many distractions so it's quite easy to concentrate on your music. I don't mean that there's nothing to do there but they aren't as fun as New York, Barcelona or London.

I started making my album at Mark Brydon's home studio. His set up was actually very similar to the one I had at home so I never really understood the point of recording at his place. On top of that he was beginning to get really busy with Moloko and the phone was ringing non-stop. It didn't work out. I could see that Mark was a nice guy and everything, but I needed to be able to concentrate 100%, not wait until he was off the phone to start a take. Steve Beckett came over to Mark's and noticed that I wasn't happy, so we moved to Red Tape studio in the centre of Sheffield.

I'd made some demos before recording and wanted to be sure I got the same sounds on the album so I brought most of my instruments over from Finland and set them up at Red Tape. In one of the shots you can see me playing the *Liberace*, which only makes very deep bass sounds. I guess it's appropriate that you can hear it making the seismic rumble in »Atlantis«.

Perhaps the most unique sounding synth was my Soviet Ritm-2, which didn't have a fully functional keyboard, but could create strange sequences if you altered the rhythm triggering the synth. My friend, Jari Lehtinen had built the trigger input and by adjusting the release time and increasing the resonance, one could control the frequency of the filter's self oscillation. This sounds complicated and I actually figured it out by turning the knobs at random. It sounded like the synth was sighing and moaning.

I'd been mostly working alone in the studio but took the opportunity to bring Ilkka Mattila over from Helsinki to record guitar. We'd been playing together since we were 16 or so and my girlfriend Tiina came over at the same time.

Helsinki, 1997

In '97 Tommi Grönlund from Sähkö heard about a talented young guy from his area and decided we should try and collaborate. The young guy was Sasse a.k.a. Freestyle Man and this was the first of many sessions we did together. He'd made a great backing track and Tommi thought we could add some live instruments on top. I played flute and some synth and we asked vibraphone virtuoso Severi Pyysalo to do a long solo. We all thought the track was good and that even if people didn't agree, they'd still be talking about the amazing vibraphone solo. The finished track was »Que Domingo Inquieto«.

   In the middle of the photo is the engineer Ari Vaahtera, who had produced all of the albums that I'd done in Finland in the 80s. I think Ari thought the music we were making there was too soft. He played in progressive rock bands and all the stuff I had made with him was industrial music. But ›Que Domingo …‹ was a huge track for all of us—especially for Sasse of course, who set up his own label after the release and started to sell a lot of records. It was more important psychologically for me because it was the first time I'd made something that was played everywhere. I remember sitting in a hotel in Osaka drinking wine with some friends when the track came on the hotel radio—it was strange to hear my music in such a mainstream setting and of course on the other side of the world.

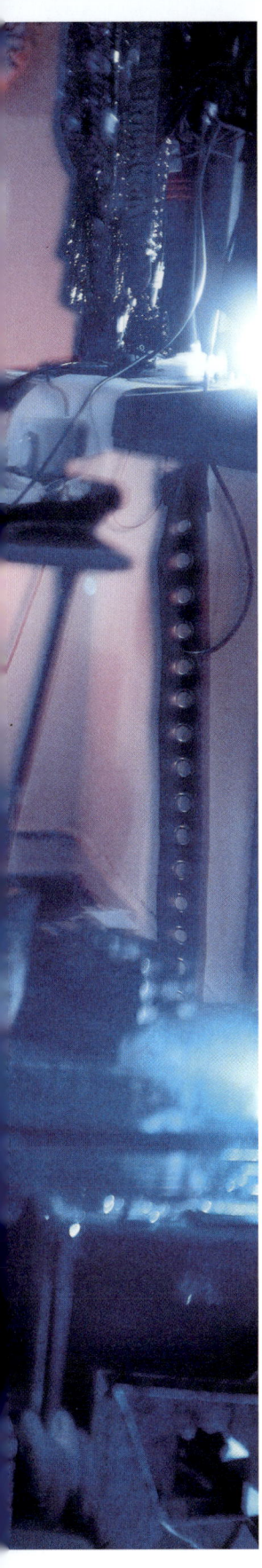

Paseo De Picasso, Barcelona, 1997

My studio was really happening in those days, it was sort of the pinnacle of my electronic music set-ups. Everything was nicely connected with midi, sync or by triggers from either 808 or 606 drum machines. I never actually owned an 808 though, the one in the picture was Tommi's, and in New York I used Can Oral's (Khan of Finland).

This is also the period when I was most obsessed with Pharoah Sanders. I loved the hippie percussion just as much as his sax and could not stop playing »Colors« with Leon Thomas on vocals. Though I had never really been that into jazz, this was a sound that I loved, so I started to collect the same kind of percussion—bells, cymbals and Moroccan drums.

On the floor you can see a C-melody saxophone I bought in New York via a second hand magazine. A C-melody is tricky to play in tune because you can't get the mouthpiece for it anymore. They were popular in the 1920s but not manufactured after that (despite a brief resurgence in the noughties), so one had to use either a tenor or alto sax mouthpiece. I chose tenor and had to push the mouthpiece really deep in the neck. Because of the tuning issues I wouldn't play the C-melody on stage, but I got a really nice sound out of it in the studio, especially when I mixed my Yamaha and the C-melody to get two different tones in the horn section.

I bought the horn from an Orthodox Jewish guy who lived in Brooklyn, not that far from Coney Island. When I went to pick it up he said; »Can I ask you? Why did you go for this unusual horn? Nobody really plays them anymore«. I think I mumbled something like »I want to try something different«. But it's true that it would be hard to play C-melody as your number one horn. The playing posture is awkward and the tuning is very peculiar.

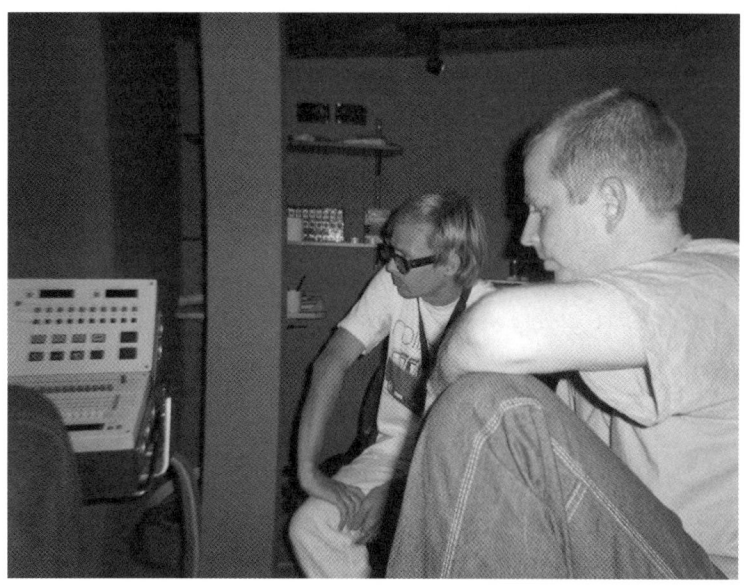

London, 1997

These images are from London. We'd been playing »Can't Stay With You Baby« in live sets for a while so Steve Beckett decided we should try and record a band version of the track. I thought it was fine, but Steve didn't think it was original enough. He had quite a clear idea of what he wanted me to sound like and obviously his instinct was right, since *Intervision* was very well received. Anyway, the band version never got used for anything in the end, which happened quite a lot in those days, especially with videos. Nowadays you can put a video on YouTube without worrying too much, but back then you needed to sell the video to a TV channel and probably pay some money to a plugger. I guess a lot of times the label didn't think it was worth it once they saw the finished video.

    Around the same time Steve and I went to see John Best, who ran a successful PR company in London. John was a busy guy and needed to be excited about his artists so I had to be ready to present myself in an interesting way. Luckily I had been around the block a couple of times and had plenty of unusual experiences to talk about. John liked me and did a great PR job.

    I was looking for a horn section for live gigs and John Best suggested Terry Edwards. I contacted Terry and funnily enough realised that I had actually met him just a couple of days earlier. He lived one block from Russell Haswell's place and they knew each other. Terry said he had a trombonist friend called Mike Kearsey and in no time we had a horn section together! Later on Mike would orchestrate and arrange most of the music on *Out of Nowhere*—I think the best collaborations tend to happen organically.

Lodz & Warzaw, 1999

For a long time I'd wanted to make an album with a symphony orchestra. I am a big fan of 20th century orchestral music by the likes of Varese, Stravinsky, Penderecki and Ligeti but in all honesty my main interest in concert music stems from watching films. I love the likes of Lalo Shifrin, Ennio Morricone, Masaru Sato, John Barry and Vangelis and would go as far as to say that film music has been the biggest inspiration on my albums. In fact, I never miss the opening titles of a movie—they are that important to me. Orchestral music is immersive in general, but even more so when it's combined with visuals in the cinema setting. Also the length of the title music appeals to me since you get all that magic and emotion in two minutes rather than the half hour of a symphony.

    I mentioned to Russell Haswell that I wanted to make this kind of album and he connected me with the noise artist Spigniew Karkowski, whose contacts included the symphony orchestra in Lodz. So, along with our tour manager Allistair, I travelled to Poland and met with the orchestra people. In those days Lodz was still quite a grim place with a similar energy to the town in a Western. The main strip looked nice, but if you went 5 steps beyond it then nothing was painted and the buildings were quite run down.

    The production of the album was complicated and I had problems with the scores. Spigniew was supposed to do the orchestration, but didn't deliver and I was in a major panic. Luckily I got in touch with Mike Kearsey who agreed to start orchestrating the material on short notice and somehow we managed to pull the project together.

    Spigniew suggested that the album needed a sitar so we hired Baluji Shrivastav and then invited a rhythm section from New York. Russell Haswell came to do some electronic impressions around the recording and Lary 7 shot the 3D photography for the cover. Last but not least, Sökö Kaukoranta, who had made the »Midsummer Night« video, came to document the recording sessions on film. This was by far the most ambitious and involved project I'd worked on, but it was nice to have so many friends around me.

The actual recording of the album was done at Warzaw radio studio. It was a grand place with a huge studio for recording orchestras. The engineer specialised in classical music, which helped a lot, but I don't think the band or orchestra were probably as well rehearsed as they needed to be. I've since learned that orchestras struggle with fast syncopated music, so perhaps this was always going to be a challenge. Unfortunately this project happened just before the digital revolution so we had to use two 24-track recorders synced by timecode and it was extremely expensive.

Despite all the setbacks, we had a great time in Lodz. It was my first time working with an orchestra and I realised it was a totally different world. It was also the first time I understood that for some people music is just a job. It was shocking to me but I have gotten used to it now and see the reasons why an 80-person orchestra needs to have a lot of discipline. In general the musicians and conductor were very friendly and fun people. They even threw a nice farewell party for us in Lodz with vodka and canapés! I think to them we were an exotic lot as well.

All in all, the project was fun but perhaps a bit too stressful for me. I think it also got me dropped from Warp because we wasted too much money. But at least I learned how to score for bigger ensembles. Quite soon after this I got a commission from UMO jazz orchestra do a concert's worth of material. That project was a success and on the *Higher Planes* album (Kitty-Yo) you can hear the tracks »Trumpcard« and »Nuclear Fusion« from a concert with them.

Lary 7's Studio, New York, 2012

Tommi from Sähkö had met Lary in New York and suggested we record some music at his studio. The studio looks completely chaotic but is famous because all his equipment was allegedly either found in the trash or salvaged from other studio closures and renovations. It's a concept studio in a way—strictly analogue with only very high-end equipment. There's an 8 track Ampex tape recorder, a monophonic 1" master tape recorder, a tube mixer from a radio station and a collection of very fancy microphones.

     Lary, Mia Theodoratus and I made a flute and harp album called *Soft Focus*. I had heard about an old Roman instrument called a *kitar*, which was commonly used to accompany poetry readings. Apparently Nero played one when he recited poems and watched Rome burn. A *kitar* doesn't have a fretboard and basically one simply strums the open strings without much change, a bit like the Indian *tamboura* or Finnish *kantele*. I wanted to make an album where a harp would play in this fashion simply to create a modal background for a solo flute or some percussion. It became quite a hypnotic album in the end and I'm hoping we can do another at some point.

Jimi's Home Studio, 2022

After sharing a studio space in Helsinki for many years, in 2016 I decided I wanted to start recording at home again. I've made most of my best material at home and one of the reasons is that I record very early in the morning, straight after that first coffee of the day. I'm still in a special state, full of energy but perhaps sometimes not quite 100% awake. I guess during the night many problems are solved in one's brain and in the morning everything is clear and you're ready to go.

I have a lot of synths and DIY instruments. Luckily there is a storage space in my building and I can keep some of my stockpile there. Though I have shelves full of them, there aren't any collector's items. All my instruments are so heavily used that they're practically worthless but I couldn't care less as long as they work for music making. Whenever I need an instrument I go and get it from the storage space and keep only the minimum in my studio. Even then the studio is a total mess. Maybe this is what creativity looks like, or it could just be the way my brain works.

Tucked away in the storage is my Yamaha SY-1, which is apparently the first synth the company made. It's a semi-preset instrument with 24 preset sounds. The sound parameters like envelope, filter and pulse width can be adjusted, so that's pretty cool. Admittedly all Yamaha synth filters leave me a little bit cold and the SY-1 is no exception, but overall this is a very reliable and useful synth. It has no low end really, so it leaves space for other instruments. The keys are great and can be touch sensitive if you want. Personally I hate touch sensitivity on synths and it is a major peeve when it's hard to turn off! I actually have another Yamaha synth in the storage. These Yamahas are solid heavy synths, so they are a bit hard to carry around. This one is some sort of a flagship model, the CS-30L. I had a Studer ¼" tape machine for years and I swapped it for this synth. This one is a wonderful piece, but very difficult to understand, so it only sees the studio on special occasions! I called the Timmion guys the day I got it and suggested we do a synth album featuring the Yamaha 30L! That project has already been recorded and is waiting to be released. Again this machine has no low end to speak of ... it's a solo synth.

In one of the studio pictures, perhaps you can see the Eko Tiger organ. This is one of the classic »surf« organs, which I bought from a flea market somewhere in Finland. I played this organ when we did the Jimi Tenor Big Band tour in 2003 and it broke every single night! The keys and the contact rods for the keys are made to break. But it was not a big issue. After each gig we collected the loose contact rods from inside the organ and soldered them back on for the following day. I love Italian organs and I especially like the Eko brand.

Some smaller bits of gear live in the linen closet next to our towels and sheets. I have a small collection of Indian electronic instruments there: a Radel tabla machine and also a tamboura machine. It seems to me that Indian music theory is not always compatible with that of the West. The Radel is programmable, but has quite strict rules about what you can do. For instance I can only put the little hand cymbals on in certain kinds of rhythms and the machine doesn't really let me program them at all. Also the tempos are really high—normally more than 200BPM. What I mean is that if the machine plays a rhythm that sounds right and original the tempo is normally around 200 or 220. I wouldn't mind this in one sense, but when I want to add the tabla machine to my own music, the programmed tempos sound half time. Normally my own music has tempos ranging from 70 to 140 or something like that. Well anyway, it's just a matter of programming my own stuff in double time. Speaking of tempos, here's something funny. I have an Oberheim DX from the seventies. The default tempo in that one is 80. All Yamaha drum machines and sequencers have a default tempo of 120. Recently I bought a Roland 808 copy. The default tempo was 140. So perhaps one day we'll catch up with India, but it might take another few decades!

    These days even a phone has a nice sequencer, but back in '94 when I got my first hardware sequencer, the Roland CSQ-100, it was a big deal. I could finally make basslines with my MS20 or make repetitive synth loops that sounded mechanical. My CSQ-100 had an extra feature though: it always added a C# in the end of the sequence. Well, I worked my way around that problem by tuning the synths to different pitches. So with my midi-free set up I had a couple of ways to make sequences. I could use the CSQ-100 or I could use the in-built sequencer in my Korg Polysix. I would typically use the chord memory function in the Polysix to get chord progressions triggered by my Korg Super percussion machine. And the third option in my early 90s studio for changing pitch was a weird one: I could make the Soviet Synth Ritm-2 change pitch if I put the filter resonance really high and cut off frequency low. Then depending on the timing that I used for triggering the synth it would play higher and lower notes. And these weren't just any notes ... they would sound very rough, almost like sounds of swallowing and grunting. You can here this sound on »Sugardaddy« and »Shore Hotel« on *Intervision*.

Because I can't record drums in my flat I can't hold certain kinds of sessions in my studio anymore, but for those sessions I book studio time. During the 2020 pandemic I even converted our summerhouse into a recording studio. We recorded the *Tenors of Kalma* album there. Drums were in the living room, the guitar amp in the kitchen and I was playing sax upstairs in the bedroom. I pulled the mic cables upstairs through a gap between the floorboards and chimney.

    If I write for big band I write the scores in my studio. I used to have a laptop as well for writing scores, but I'm not so crazy about writing music when I travel. Anyway I prefer writing scored music at home. I have my instruments there and I can jam. I want to get into the mood of the song, improvise horn arrangements with sax or flute and later transcribe them on paper. This is a method that suits me. I know a lot of good composers hear the music in their head and write it down just like that, but not me. I need to test things, make mistakes. And also if I use synths the slightest change of a filter might change the mood of the composition and I would try to find a new way to write it. I always try to follow this new path if I stumble upon it. I don't have any remorse discarding material that I have worked on all day or even days if the new, accidental direction has revealed itself.

people

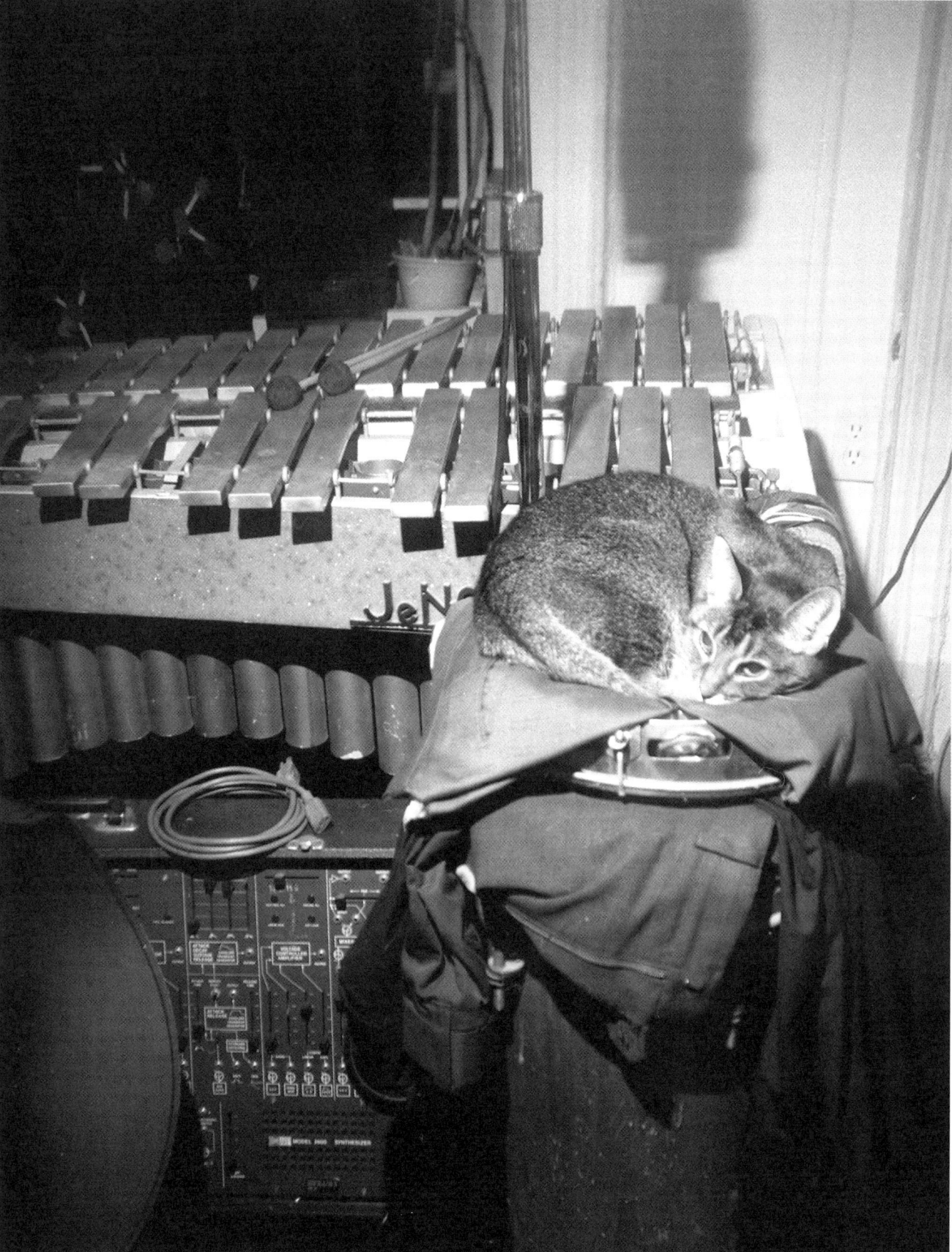

Lary 7

Yeah, Lary is a legend. In his own words he's the last remaining artist in his neighbourhood. He lives on the corner of Avenue B and 2nd Street, right where the Gas Station used to be. The Gas Station was actually an abandoned gas station, which had an outdoor statue park. Inside there was a bar where legendary underground events took place. From the street it really looked like a wasteland. In the 80s and even the early 90s, when you walked down to the corner store there might be a Latin group playing in front of the deli. It was happening! Now the area is expensive and the artists are almost all gone.

His house is a piece of art by itself. Packed to the rafters with electronics, antiques and artwork, his flat is so full you can hardly find a place to put down a drink—at least the cat managed to find a spot to rest. Amongst the treasure trove of audio-visual equipment there are a couple of camera lenses made by Carl Zeiss Jena. Some of the Jena lenses were made out of a type of quartz which is perfect for a lens, but slightly radioactive. Lary used to keep these lenses by his bed, until his brother, a doctor, told him to store them elsewhere. He also has a large percussion collection. As well as tubular bells in his kitchen, he has several sets of glockenspiels, a vibraphone and loads of bamboo percussion. He's a big fan of exotica so these kinds of instruments come handy for that type of sound.

Tommi and I collaborated many times with Lary 7, both in New York and elsewhere. When we were both living in Barcelona, Tommi organised a club night at a bar in the old town, where he would DJ and Lary would play live. Lary brought an old drum machine, opened it up and used a piece of tin foil to make new connections between the microchips. Basically he was circuit bending. This sound didn't go down well with the owner during the soundcheck and he asked us to cancel the gig, positive the night would be a disaster. We managed to persuade him to let the gig happen and afterwards he came to us and exclaimed: »What a success, so many people left the live room and came to the bar to drink during the show. We made a lot of money«

Russell Haswell

I'm into food. Whether it's fancy food, home cooking, street food or sometimes junk food, I like to eat it all. While I was signed to Warp I spent a lot of time in London, especially when the label moved there from Sheffield in 1999. If I was in the city I usually ended up in Whitechapel, often staying at Russell Haswell's place. In this picture we are at a place called Don Pepe's. It was Whitechapel's finest greasy spoon. I think I always got the full English breakfast, which was the perfect antidote to our frequent hangovers.

Whitechapel was happening at that time. There were a lot of art openings and more often than not we were invited. I like art openings. I like cocktail parties as well! Russell would normally buy the Frieze magazine from the Whitechapel gallery and read all the articles. It seemed to me that he knew everything there was to know about contemporary art. Well, later on he did get a job at P.S.1. as a curator, so I guess I was right!

Russell was also an expert in noise music and metal. Not all metal but the darker sub-genres of metal I would say. I learned a lot about music from him. He introduced me to Boredoms, Earth, Aphex Twin, Autechre, Electric Wizard, Messonna and LFO for example. And the interesting part is that he not only introduced me to the music but to the people as well.

The first time I met Russell was when we played a Sähkö gig at Fridge in Brixton in 1994. He was in the audience with Paul Smith and they liked our show. Ilpo Väisänen was doing his noise workout with his special »typewriter« synth. Ilpo's extreme noise was too much for the PA and he ended up blowing the fuse for the whole building, and that was the end of our gig. We had only played for about 7 minutes. Even so, Paul Smith was impressed and came to talk to us after the show about a record deal. I was like »No, no, we are Sähkö artists. We can't be signed to other labels«, but we took his card anyway. Back in Finland Tommi Grönlund talked about the card to Mika Vainio and of course he recognised that Paul was the legendary guy from Blast First. After some discussion Tommi and Mika agreed that perhaps Ilpo and Mika's Panasonic could be signed to Blast First. It ended up being a great deal for all of us. We started to spend a lot of time hanging out with Paul Smith, Susan Stenger, Russell Haswell and Bruce Gilbert. I remember those as really happy times. We all went to Bruce's 50th birthday and I also ended up playing at Paul & Sue's wedding in 2000.

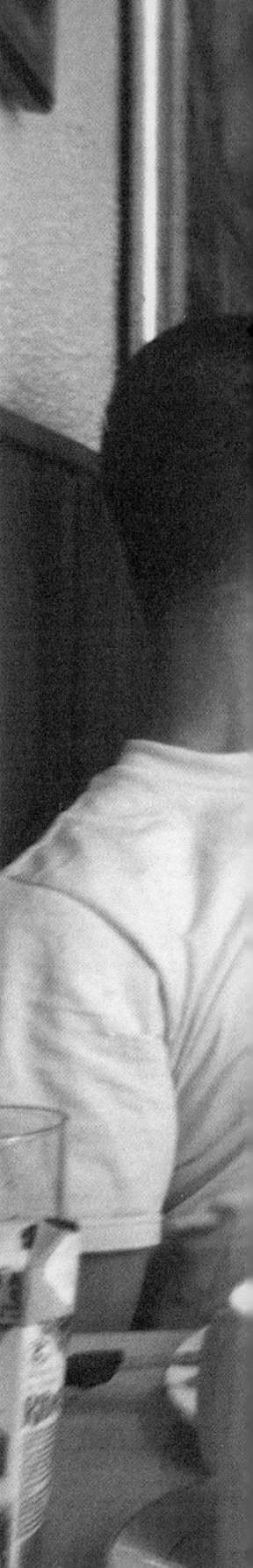

When I moved to Barcelona in 1996, Russell would come and visit quite often. We would hang out with Sergio Caballero and the Sónar people. In fact Russell and I ended up travelling together a lot in the late 90s. We visited the Mego people in Vienna several times and went to Japan together when I had some gigs there. During that trip we saw Boredoms perform at the university of Osaka. Yamantaka Eye's leg was in a cast but he spent the whole two hours jumping around like crazy while they played two long psychedelic tracks. Afterwards we went backstage, which was one of the classrooms in the university, and he was lying on a desk, holding his leg and wailing about how much it hurt. I guess with all the adrenaline he hadn't noticed during the gig, or else he's just a consummate professional—either way, the man had really suffered for his art, because it turned out he'd originally hurt his leg falling off stage at another show. I'm thankful for his sacrifice though because that was a truly amazing performance.

Nicole Willis

In 1999 I was invited to New York to show the videos I'd made for Warp and Viva TV in Cologne. I had some gigs over there at the same time, maybe at the Bell Jazz Festival or something, and since there were plenty of other Warp and Sähkö people in town, we all hung out. I met Nicole at one of these gatherings and soon after we tried to make a track at her house. That first collaboration was promising so we decided to work on a full album for Sähkö, which Maurice Fulton and I would produce. That record was called *Soul Makeover*. We started the recording sessions at my studio in Barcelona and finished them in New York at Maurice's place. One thing led to another and Nicole and I got married in New York later that year. Russell Haswell was one of the witnesses and our wedding party was at a Karaoke bar in Chinatown. We were married for 16 years and have two kids.

    Nicole and I made many albums over those 16 years, and collaborated with the likes of Tony Allen, The Soul Investigators and the UMO Helsinki Jazz Orchestra, the latter of which spawned the hit song, »Still Got A Way To Fall«. I also took the cover photo for Nicole's *Tortured Soul* album with The Soul Investigators. I had heard about the technique which Curtis used to take his pictures of Indigenous Americans and wanted to give it a try, so I built a black tent on our balcony and let light in from one side. I think it worked out fine! This was originally a digital colour shot, but I primarily used the blue channel in order to imitate orthochromatic film.

    I love film, but I'm not a purist who won't use digital under any circumstances. If you want a certain look it's way easier to get good results with film, especially if you use special techniques like shooting directly on paper or using a wet plate. Actually I guess wet plate isn't even considered film. It's convenient to take pictures with a phone and these days one can get wonderful results but there is still a place for large format cameras and film. I suppose one could compare using an old camera to playing a Hammond organ or a classical wooden flute. There is something really special about them, which can't be replicated by modern technology.

The Soul Investigators

In 2002, we were sent a CD-r of dirty funk tracks by The Soul Investigators, which I initially found underwhelming. At the time lots of people were sampling old funk tracks, and I mistakenly thought this was just another one of those unoriginal projects. But when I realised that they were a live band I was beyond impressed—I couldn't believe that they'd achieved such an authentic sound and impeccable groove.

The Soul Investigators asked Nicole if she wanted to record a song with them and sent their producer Didier Selin to Barcelona with the multitrack tape. We went uptown to a studio that was run by a Canadian guy called Peter and did our thing. The recording went well and Nicole ended up doing three albums with the Soul Investigators, the first of which, *Keep Reaching Out* has since become a bit of a classic.

I was very impressed by the sound and production of *Keep Reaching Out*, so much so that I asked Didier Selin to produce the Jimi Tenor and Kabukabu album. We happened to have a gig at the Koneisto festival in Helsinki at the same warehouse complex where the Timmion studio was situated, so we had our first recording sessions there during the festival.

What I love about working with Timmion (the label and studio run by The Soul Investigators) is that they keep the studio set up the same whenever it's possible. Once they find a good drum sound, they don't change anything. This reminds me of Studio One in Jamaica and I think it's a wise way to go. You can waste half of your life looking for a perfect snare sound ... and I think if you try so hard to find the sound, you'll never quite get it!

Later on I was often a member of the horn section when The Soul Investigators recorded their albums with Nicole. They were fun sessions. We shared many of the same ideas about recording and especially recording horns. Recently I've been working with Timmion on a regular basis as a horn player in studio sessions. We've also worked on my solo album material there, which will hopefully be out someday soon.

Tony Allen

When my three-album deal with Warp ended in 2003 I signed to Kitty-Yo. I met the whole crew in Berlin and instantly knew that they were wonderful people. One of the tracks I was working on at the time needed a Latin rhythm so I asked the label boss Raik Hölzel if he knew any Latin players. While he was busy checking his Rolodex, I noticed that Tony Allen was living in Europe and had just released a new album, *Black Voices*, and decided that maybe we could get him to play on my track instead of a Latin rhythm section. Raik knew a DJ called Armin Engel from a Berlin jazz radio station and asked him if he knew Tony Allen. Armin was in contact with Tony, but unfortunately he was busy or something and couldn't do it. So Armin put me in touch with an African band based in Berlin called Rhythm Taxi, featuring some of the members of Fela's Africa 70. I ended up working with Rhythm Taxi (who were later called Kabukabu) for many years and still work with some of the members now.

A few years later, Quinton Scott from Strut contacted me about a series of releases called *Inspiration Information*, asking if I'd be interested in contributing. The idea of the series was that one contemporary musician would suggest five older artists they'd like to work with and then Strut would find out which »inspiration« would be available for the project. Tony Allen was on my list and luckily he agreed to do it.

We decided to record at Lovelite in Berlin, a small studio in a garage-style room next to the club of the same name in Friedrichshain. I met Tony at the studio and it was kind of awkward at first since he didn't know who I was or what we were going to do. I had made demos in advance and planned to do a percussion album with a few horns on top. The musicians were Ekow Alabi Savage, Akinola Famson, Daniel Allen Oberto and Momo Diafone. The label had hired a photographer and we had to pose together for press shots even though we hadn't played a single note and were still complete strangers.

It was quite tense, so we did the sensible thing and went for some lunch. After a good meal and some good wine the ice was broken and the whole project started to flow nicely. Tony wanted to have guitar and bass so we quickly hired some players. This meant the word got out that Tony Allen was in the studio, so plenty of people started to arrive to pay their respects to the legend. The album was a success and we did a few tours afterwards, enlisting Allonymous to do vocals. We had a great time.

Tony had his 70th birthday concert at the Barbican Centre and I was invited as one of the soloists, which was really amazing for me. There were so many wonderful people involved, like PW Ellis and Seun Kuti; Byron Wallen was the musical director and Ogene Kologbo played guitar. Pee Wee Ellis asked me to join him on the saxophone backings for Cheikh Lo—I was in seventh heaven all right!

Soon after the Barbican performance I had a project with UMO Jazz Orchestra in Finland and asked Tony to play drums. I think this was the first time he played with a big band and he took to it immediately. Afterwards I suggested that he should try to get a big band in France to do his material, and sure enough he put it together with David Murray doing the arrangements. I never managed to catch the show live but heard it was great.

Some years later my friend Paul Smith organised a Moog event at Ace Hotel in London and asked if Tony and I could do a special performance using Moog gear. At the time I'd been developing a triggering system for percussion, so that when the drummer hits a drum, a sequencer tells a synthesizer to play a note. a sound engineer Finlay Shakespeare made special devices for this purpose and so we hooked up Tony's drums to all these sequencers and Moogs. I had prepared the sequences in advance with basslines for the kick drum, three note harmonies for the snare and high pitched ostinatos for the hi-hat. It sounded amazing and strange—Tony couldn't believe it! We played two gigs with the system at Café Oto in London—it was a crazy night!

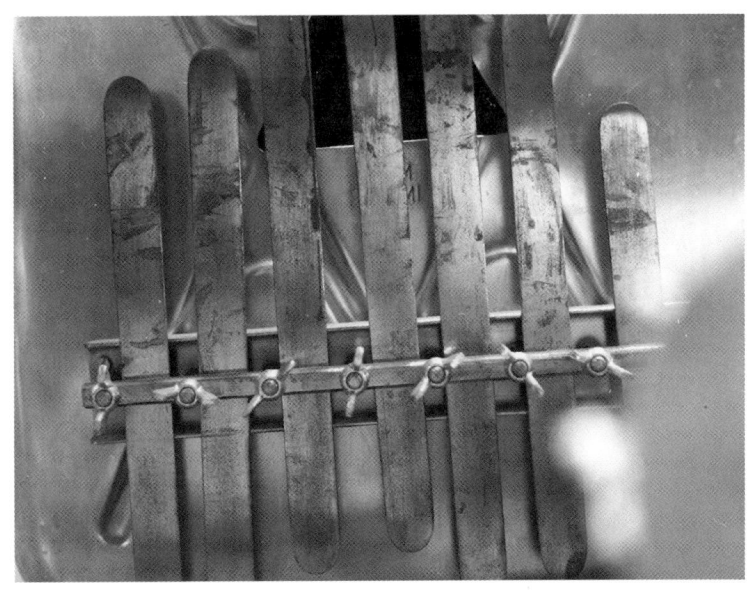

Itetune

Itetune is a band that plays only DIY instruments. The project was originally just Abdissa Assefa and I recording our primitive homemade instruments on multitrack equipment, but later on we hired extra musicians to help out in the live gigs. Abdissa is a big session musician in Finland and we met naturally at some festival or other. We both love food and bonded at barbecues and cookouts over the following years. As we got to know each other better and realised we both had all these crazy homemade instruments, it just made sense to play them together. Abdissa is more specialised in percussion, while I create the wind and electro-mechanical elements. I guess it's needless to say that all Itetune songs are composed by Itetune!

The word »ite« comes from a Finnish word that means »self« in English. In Finland outsider art is quite popular and it has a special name *Itetaide*, which translates as »self-art«. I'm quite into outsider art. My favorite outsider artist in Finland is Veijo Rönkkönen and I took the cover shot for *Higher Planes* at his statue park by his home near the Russian border. That photo shows his most famous work, around one hundred self-portrait statues in various yoga positions all facing the morning sun. They're quite crudely shaped out of concrete and now, at about thirty years old, completely covered in moss and lichen. The sculptures are kind of haunting and uncanny, especially since he used old false teeth and dentures in the mouths. I think one statue, *Javelin Thrower*, even has his father's old false teeth.

For our first album, also called *Itetune*, we took the cover pictures with a homemade pinhole camera and then the label guy, Roope Seppälä printed the sleeves himself using a silk-screen on second hand covers, which he had collected from flea markets. On top of everything, each one of the 150 vinyl copies was individually cut on a special lathe. It almost drove the cutting engineer crazy, though that happened to be Roope too. I guess everything about the release was DIY!

Kabukabu

I first met the Kabukabu guys backstage at a Kitty-Yo label night at Volksbühne. I had recently worked with Mikey Wilson who played on »Call of The Wild« and »Better Than Ever« on my *Out of Nowhere* album so he was playing with me that night. Normally I would have had Chris Dawkins in my band as well, but he couldn't make it that time. Angela Bulloch, one of the Young British Artists was there. I knew Angela quite well through Rusell Haswell and since her boyfriend was a promoter at Volksbühne, she came over.

Kabukabu was still called Rhythm Taxi then. Their concept was that Rhythm Taxi was like a cab that you could hire if you needed an African rhythm group. My first attempt to collaborate with Tony Allen had just fallen through, so Armin Engel suggested I hail the Rhythm Taxi. I had never worked with musicians from Africa before and it was very exciting. At that time Rhythm Taxi was Nicholas Addo-Nettey and Oghene Kologbo from Fela's Africa 70, Sometimer on bass, Ekow Alabi Savage on drums and Akinola Famson on percussion.

We ended up playing loads of gigs together over the years and at some point they changed their name to Kabukabu (which is also a kind of taxi, a converted minivan that seats about 9 people). We made the first album in 2006 at the Timmion studio in Helsinki then recorded most of our other stuff at Lovelite in Berlin. Jochen Ströh was the engineer at Lovelite and he gradually turned the studio into a recording mecca for African music. Plenty of people have played with Kabukabu during the years at my gigs—loads of horn players, percussionists, guitar players and bassists. It's a tough job to keep large groups together.

In 2008 we played a great gig at a packed Jazz Café in London. Nicholas Addo-Nettey was full of energy that night. We had taken a lot of *Joystone* albums on the tour but Nicholas sold them all on the first night at Jazz Café! I remember him coming backstage several times with his hands full of money and pouring it on the table before running back downstairs to sell more. We got a review in a London newspaper from that gig describing our sound as »hooligan jazz«. We liked that and afterwards if people asked what genre of music we were playing our answer was always »Hooligan Jazz«.

In 2012 we played on an artificial island in Estonia. A man who used to work for Estonian TV creates artificial lakes every year at his holiday resort and arranges special performances. We played in the middle of the largest lake, about 300m from the shore, but since the PA was in front of the crowd at the resort we could only hear the music from the monitors on the island. After each song we got the applause from the mainland with a little delay. The line up at this place is mostly made up of ambient or esoteric artists who don't really rely on the energy of the audience as much, so it was a strange gig for us. Nevertheless it was a great experience!

Max Weissenfeldt

I met Max Weissenfeldt in a small town outside Berlin called Eberswalde in May 2015, when I was supporting the Pyramids with Tenors of Kalma. At that time I think Max was very keen to work with the Pyramids. He must have been keen to work with me too as he approached me at the gig and asked if I would be interested in making a 7" for Philophon. I thought it sounded like a good idea, especially if I could bring Ekow Alabi Savage along to the sessions.

The 7" went really well and Max suggested that we carry on collaborating. Gradually we ended up making an album's worth of material and it soon became *Order of Nothingness*. Since the album was a relative success it felt natural to make a follow up, so I went to Berlin to record more tracks at Max's Joy Sound Studios, which is a magical place piled high with percussion! There was even a full gamelan set there, but we were not allowed to touch them since they belonged to a gamelan master who was now too old to play them.

On *Order Of Nothingness* we found a good working process, starting each track with the rhythm section. Ekow and Max would play drums and percussion and I would play bass with a WLM organ. For some reason we changed our process a little when we were working on *Aulos*, and even though we recorded a lot of tracks, none of them worked out. I think we recorded for more than a week and still didn't get any results. Naturally I was a bit depressed. After listening to all the material, Max called me and said that there was nothing usable for the next album.

We took a couple of months off and I made a few new demos. The demos were better than the previous session so we decided to give it another try and things finally started to work out. We made another two tracks, »Vocalize My Love« and »Ki'igba«, with Florence Adooni and Lizzy Amaliyenga and before we knew it there seemed to be enough material for the second album.

While we were recording, Max was also in the process of moving his whole operation to Kumasi in Ghana and in fact mixed the album there. Since *Aulos* is a kind of Greek flute, we thought it might be fun to have flute interludes on there, so I recorded some solo pieces and sent them over. Max ended up recording a local percussionist on top of the solos and it sounded great. It's proof that long distance collaborations can work.

Petri »Pete« Toikkanen

One of the things I liked most about The Soul Investigators was the guitar, which had the rare quality of being super tight but totally laid back at the same time—one of the essential ingredients of groove music. Strange then that their guitarist was always replaced by a session player when I saw them live. It turned out that the man in question is a notorious alcoholic called Pete Toikkanen, who was such a difficult character that the band didn't want to play with him anymore.

I chatted to the Timmion guys and they said that despite his addiction, Pete is still a genius and perhaps I should get him into the studio for writing sessions. So that's what happened. He has been at the studio on and off for a number of years now, contributing a lot to a couple of Nicole Willis albums, including Nicole Willis with UMO Jazz Orchestra on which he is a co-writer for all the songs.

He also had a band called Haunted by Hallucinations and Nicole and I decided to record and release their album on our label Herakles. This was my first real experience of producing another band and it had plenty of new challenges for me. Nicole and I co-produced the album. The sessions were kind of chaotic and if we started early enough we could maybe get in a good hour while Pete wasn't too drunk. Unfortunately we didn't start early that often as he struggled to wake up. If we didn't get results on the first few takes, he'd end up shouting and swearing at the rest of the band. I learned that to be a producer, people skills are probably more important than technical skills. You spend a lot of time managing personalities and trying to keep everyone happy. This is a PR shot for that album—and also cigarette butts from his kitchen.

Maurice Fulton

When I was in Barcelona I lived at Paseo de Picasso and this was the small courtyard we had out back. It was all concrete and quite brutal but it was still outdoors and you could drink coffee and eat there. We were recording with Maurice around this time. We always ended up recording something when we met.

On one of these occasions we were making a track that was very erotic and romantic. Since Paris is the city of love, we decided that the track needed female vocals in French! I knew Emmanuelle who was married to my friend Sergio Caballero from Sónar festival and we asked her to say something sultry on the track. She asked us to be more specific and Maurice immediately came up with lines like: »Let's go to a fine restaurant, have a table with candle light and drink red wine«. I was like »c'mon we need to be more subtle than that! Let's try to work out some kind of metaphor or something.« But no, straight away Emmanuelle recited Maurice's lyrics in French and they stuck. Before we knew it »C'était Bon, Très Bon« was complete and we put it out on Puu under the name Hot Sauce.

We figured out a funny thing while doing that track: Emmanuelle said a special French word that is simply inhaling quickly through your mouth—the sound of rushing air going in. And amazingly in Finnish we have the same word! In Finnish it means ›yes‹. I think in French it has a different meaning.

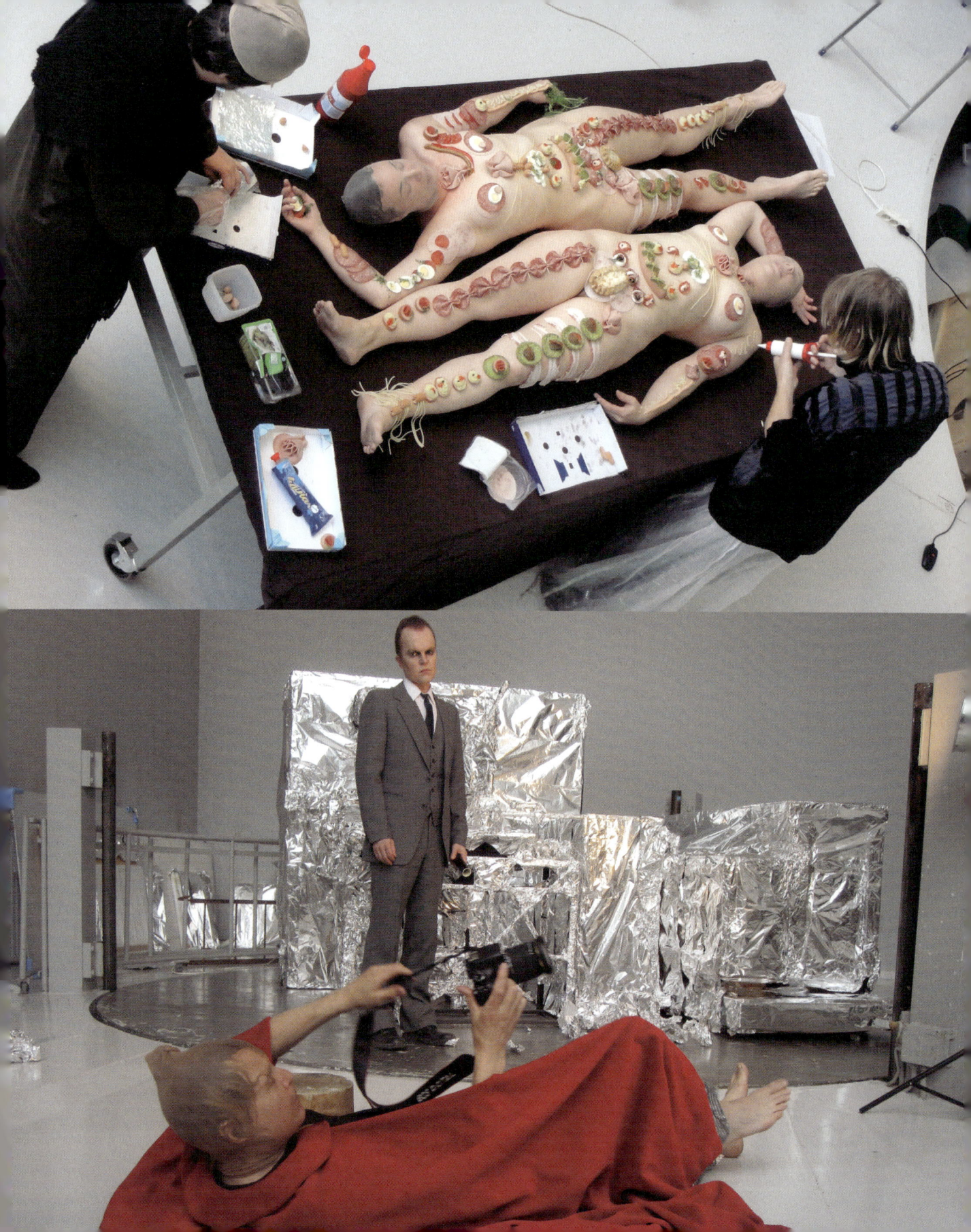

Jori Hulkkonen

Jori Hulkkonen and I have been live scoring *Sähkö-the Movie* for many years. We take the original soundtrack away and play a totally new soundtrack live, made from mostly improvised electronic music. But in 2014 we decided that instead of creating a score for a film which already exists, we could make a totally new film for live performance purposes. And on top of that, make a film which is never the same twice. We could keep changing the material as we go, and since the film would never be released, it would have to be seen live or not at all. Also the music could be different at every performance.

    Jori had met a guy called Mr Normall backstage at a John Foxx gig in London, when someone told him that there was another Finnish person there. Now, Mr Normall goes to 80s synth pop gigs on a regular basis and has the typical new romantic style with lots of make-up and a smart suit. We thought we could make a sci-fi movie starring Mr Normall as himself—he had a great look and who knows, maybe he could act. The science in our science fiction would be so advanced that we wouldn't need many special effects. Everything would look natural because it's so far beyond what we can imagine. *Nuntius* is a sci-fi road movie, so we just drove around Finland scouting for outlandish locations and then started shooting straight away. We had a slim storyline to work from, but plenty of room for improvisation.

    I'm a big fan of surrealist films and photography. I especially like the fact that those films were made by artists and were normally based on improvised ideas or some clever visual tricks that didn't require a huge production. In some ways I think it can be compared to jazz or any improvised music. Huge productions don't necessarily help in jazz, and actually could be a hindrance ... If you have an OK recording, you're good. Jori had a Canon camera and I had some good lenses, so we were ready to go.

    In the autumn of 2014 we had the first version of the film ready and we have been performing it around the world since. Düsseldorf, Barcelona, Bangkok, Warsaw, Helsinki, St Petersburg, Reykjavik. We've made 3 different versions of the film so far and I hope we can do some more in the future.

Matti Knaapi

During my time at the Oulunkylä jazz school, a classmate played bass in an art school party band called Honey Productions. When they needed an extra player in their horn section I volunteered, and quickly became firm friends with their other guitarist, Matti Knaapi.

Matti studied industrial design, and at the time I was making industrial noise music with the Shamans. We were due to perform live on Finnish TV soon and I wanted something special and memorable to be built for the performance. My vision was a big windmill-like drum machine and I asked Matti if he'd help me bring it to life. He was still enrolled at the art school and so we could use their metal workshop to construct it. After a couple of prototypes we arrived at the finished Sirkka, and you can read more about that wonderful machine later.

Since then Matti and I have collaborated on numerous projects. We've made more drum machines, a noise box inspired by Luigi Russolo, a theremin-like instrument called the »Photophone« and »Liberace«, a bass keyboard for DJs. He has also helped me create the backdrops and stage sets for my live performances, and in a sense the shows are often a group effort.

I have lots of ideas for unusual instrument designs, but lack the necessary technical know-how. On the other hand Matti is a professional industrial designer and runs a software company so he has an encyclopaedic knowledge of fabrication and manufacture. We come at problems from two different directions and so it's a very natural collaboration. We do a lot of brainstorming together and have exchanged thousands of emails over the years about more or less everything, literally! Our favourite topics so far have been: sour dough bread, the structure of the cosmos, Japanese pickles, acoustic overtones, mushrooms and the making of spirits ... I guess we're modern day alchemists really.

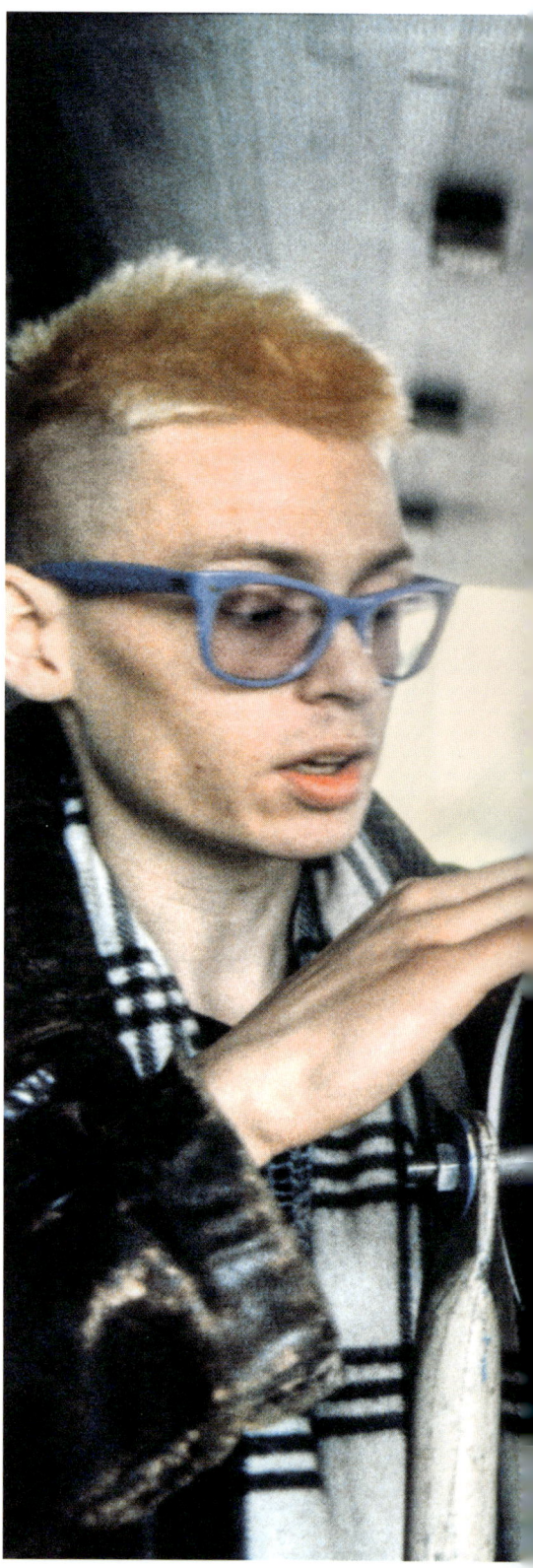

Actions

Crane Show, Urban Rock, Helsinki, 1988

In Finland in the eighties the idea of an urban music festival was totally new. There had been loads of festivals in the countryside but never one in the city. Urban Rock was Teemu Lehto's idea and he wanted Jimi Tenor and his Shamans to do something really wild. In 1983 our mutual friend Matti Knaapi had done a ballet for construction cranes and by '88 Jimi Tenor and his Shamans had played gigs in all sorts of industrial locations. The natural conclusion was to stage a performance hanging from a crane. The music was sent via a radio connection to the PA set on the ground.

It was a great moment when we were lifted from the ground up to the sky. The whole street was full of people who couldn't quite figure out what we were planning to do. But once we were up there it was strange—kind of lonely. We could hear echoes of our music from the PA with a great delay. Furthermore, we had a generator up there to power our equipment, and its mechanical chug made it even harder to hear ourselves.

Musically, we stuck to our regular setlist. We had faith in the material, but our recordings weren't that good. I guess we hoped that these interesting live shows would help people connect with our sound and lead to something bigger. It was hard to get noticed back then, not like today when a video can spread everywhere immediately.

The idea of hanging from a crane over the city was definitely inspired by the famous butoh dancers hanging by ropes from a skyscraper. Teemu Lehto's original idea was that we would be hanging from theatrical harnesses and going up and down in the air. I have a respectable fear of heights and for me that was just a little too much.

Sähkö Tour, Glasgow, 1994

By 1994 Mika's first Ø EP and my *Sähkömies* LP had come out. Soon enough we were contacted by JD Twitch, who wanted to release »Take Me Baby« as a 12" single and perhaps do some remixes. This was exciting news but there was a slight technical hitch—when I made »Take Me Baby« I didn't have a multitrack and actually recorded it to a hi-fi VHS tape. There was a new version of VHS tape recorders that had a digital soundtrack, and the recorder I used also had a very nice limiter so worked perfectly as a master tape recorder. But since I didn't have a separate vocal track of »Take Me Baby« the remixes would have to be totally recreated including the vocal take.

    JD Twitch ran a club called Pure in Glasgow and Edinburgh and invited us to perform there, which gave us the opportunity to put together a small Sähkö tour of the UK. Mika Vainio was too nervous to go on that tour and so the line up was Ilpo Väisänen, Kim Rapatti and I. During the tour, I ended up recording a version of »Take Me Baby« in somebody's kitchen, and eventually the remix EP was released by T&B vinyl.

    That trip to the UK was crucial for us and we made plenty of friends and contacts. Panasonic signed for Blast First / Mute because we met Paul Smith after a gig in Brixton, we met Jill Mingo who went on to do Sähkö PR for many years, and I got half of my Sähkö movie filmed during the trip. We've played at Pure and Optimo several times during the years. When I showed Sähkö the Movie at the Glasgow Short Film Festival in 2015 we did a Q&A with JD Twitch after the screening, and now he's been kind enough to write the foreword for this book!

Tenorwear, Sala Apolo, 1997

I once read an article in an underground fanzine about a Finnish producer/musician called Jimi Sumén, who explained that his trousers had really long zippers on the sides of the leg which allowed him to change their shape. This seemed like a great idea so I asked my friends who ran a fashion store to make a similar pair for myself. My pants could be changed in a couple of seconds to be either baggy, flare or straight so no matter how the fashions changed these pants would always be always cool!

When I was wearing these special trousers on the dance floor in a club in London, several people came to ask where I'd bought them and it suddenly occurred to me that perhaps I should start a fashion line. Fashion looked like a glamorous business and I liked the idea of the cocktail parties, but wasn't too interested in the actual designing. I thought I could outsource that to other people and just be the figurehead, which is exactly what the huge US stars have been doing since the 2010s. Well, I didn't have any pro people behind me so after a few years the project got too tedious to run.

Despite these drawbacks, we did manage to do a »legendary« catwalk show at the Sala Apolo in Barcelona, using mostly transvestites from the Ramblas as models. Sergio Caballero and I would go to the bars where the transvestites hung out in the evenings and try to persuade them to come and model for the show. Fortunately they were well up for it and I set up a photo studio backstage. It was a lot of fun and allowed all of us to get our glamorous 15 minutes of fame experience. Maurice Fulton played records for the show and my girlfriend Tiina modelled an A-shape skirt which I'd made from a painting I bought in the flea market.

The last models on stage were Tommi Grönlund and Harri Hännikäinen who were dressed in these huge transparent plastic bags, which were spray painted with the Tenorwear logo and hanging from hula-hoops on their shoulders. Under the plastic they had no clothes on and you could clearly see that they were naked. In all honesty they looked terrible! Presumably hoping to cope with the embarrassment, Tommi and Harri got so drunk that they became lost in the venue and for a full five minutes there was nothing happening on stage. In the end they stumbled in front of the crowd quite obviously trashed out of their minds. Later on the audience said they had never seen a less professional fashion show—Yeah!

Backdrop, Barcelona, 1998

When I was 16 I went to a colour theory class in my local camera club and became very interested in primary colours and how they work. Around the same time, my art teacher showed us her new landscape paintings, which were made using only cyan, magenta and yellow, and a short time later I read about James Clerk Maxwell's theory of colour photography. Since then, I've always been obsessed with colour theory and have incorporated it into my photography, artwork and stage design many times over the years.

At one point, Matti Knaapi and I constructed a special backdrop for Jimi Tenor and His Shamans that used RGB colours. We painted a huge cogwheel where the cogs were painted in red, green or blue. When the lights on stage changed between these colours, the cogwheel appeared to be rotating.

I had seen a performance in a Steiner school in Berlin where they had a special Steiner-stage, which was painted grey. The grey stage would neatly become whatever colour was used for the stage lights. After this I revisited the idea, and for Sónar 98 we made a big painting that looked like a colour-blindness test. We would use red, green and blue dots only. Depending on the general lights on stage the painting would have a different image. Though I never get to see the results of the backdrops as I'm facing the crowd and focussing on the gig, the staging is always a group effort and Matti is always in the audience to check the results.

In the late 1990s and early 2000s I ended up taking several photos for record sleeves that were colour photos, but taken with black and white film. I used primary colour filters (red, green and blue) when shooting the pictures. This technique requires three exposures of the same subject, so it was important not to move at all. I combined these monochromatic images on computer by putting them in different colour channels. The end result was a colour photo. When you shoot outside there is always some movement and the individual layers don't match perfectly, but that's what makes this technique interesting.

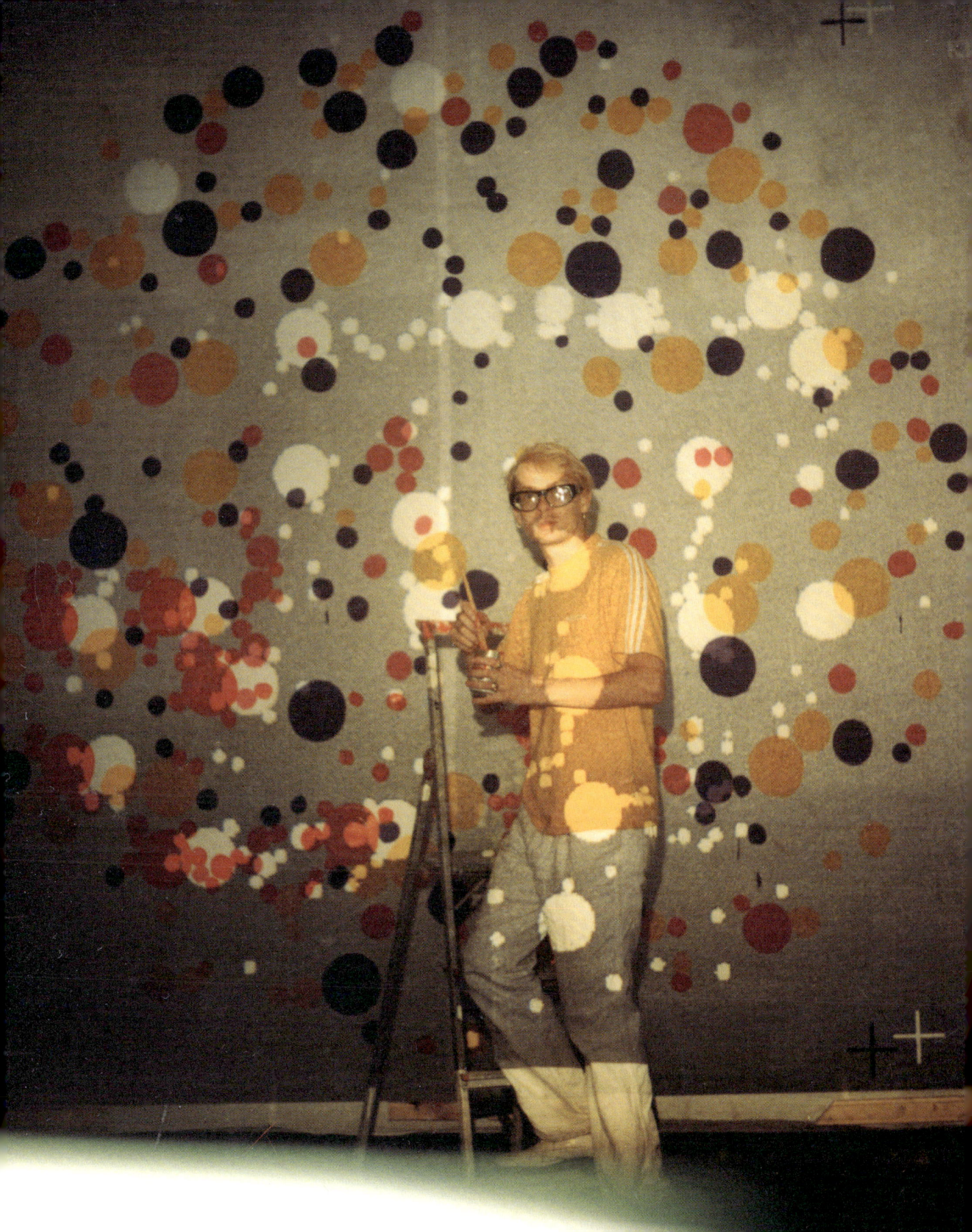

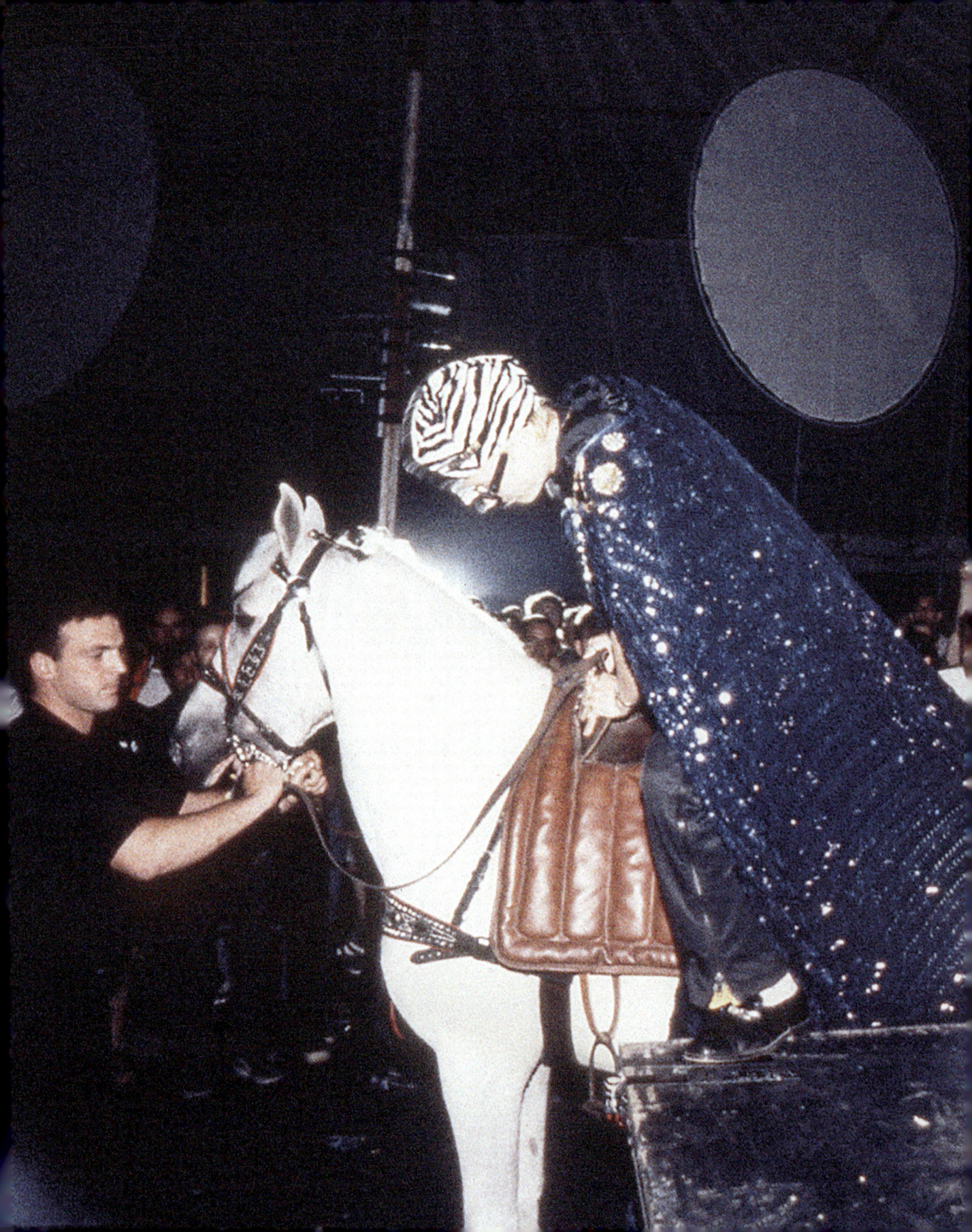

Sónar Festival, Barcelona, 1998

After I signed with Warp in 1996 I left the communist party dancehall in Espoo and moved to Barcelona. At that time I had far too much energy and I thought I could do everything all at once. I'd started the Tenorwear fashion label, continued to take pictures, made my own instruments and wrote and recorded new music for the Warp deal.

Soon enough I became friends with Sergio Caballero, who was one of the organisers of Sónar-festival. I invited him and some other friends to my house for a party, which involved me making an action painting using food colouring and yoghurt. Sergio really liked the idea of action painting and suggested that I do a special show at Sónar 98, which would include all of my interests at that time. As well as a fashion show, theatrical stage ideas and DIY instruments, Sergio wanted me to ride to the stage on horseback and end the show with a firework display.

Musically, the setlist focused on songs from my album *Organism*, and Terry Edwards, Chris Dawkins and Maurice Fulton were my band for the night. The band was playing »Take Me Baby« when I was riding through the audience on horseback. When I finally made it on stage I started the vocals. We had cut some dubplates of my rhythm tracks and Maurice was on the decks. I also had my solo show set-up there; Oberheim DX drum machine, Korg MS20, Yamaha sequencer and a Farfisa organ. In those days I was really into soft and sensual music. We did play faster tracks too, but I kind of had to force myself to do them. It was one of the first times I played with Chris Dawkins and he would end up playing with me regularly until 2004.

Every song had a different theme and a stage set; we even had a bartender on stage as one of the performers. Matti Knaapi had flown from Finland and he brought a special backdrop machine constructed by Enver Mäkelä in the cargo hold of the plane. The backdrop machine had 5 different backdrops and it would change them between the songs. There was a glitter curtain, a sunset by the seashore and an image of a jazz orchestra where the players were the same size as me on the stage (this one was great for solo gigs!).

For the song »Love and Work«, our set designer Roland Olbeter had made a special pink cushioned bed and I lay down to sing, trying my best to move erotically.

In the end there was a fashion extravaganza and I had my transvestite models from La Rambla performing again. We bought disposable paper suits for them and at the very end of the show I action painted their bodies with coloured liquids on the catwalk. At that moment there was supposed to be fireworks, but something went wrong and they didn't work. A friend of mine, Anatole Kysk, was working on stage costumes in Paris and I asked him to design a blue sequined cape for my grand entrance. It also covered most of the horse, and was very beautiful. I actually went all the way to the fabric district in Paris to buy the sequin material. Sadly the official photographer showed up too late to the gig and didn't manage to get any pictures, but at least one photo of me on horseback did make it into the Sónar book.

Afterparty, Barcelona, 1998

After the mixed media extravaganza on the Sónar stage, Chris and I played at one of the many unofficial parties around the festival. Tommi Grönlund was the man who connected people and organised parties, and this particular event was at one of the kiosks on Barcelona beach. Unfortunately the city stopped allowing this kind of party quite soon after this, which was a real shame, as the kiosk parties were our favourite thing about the city. Mika Vainio mostly played Jamaican dub and rocksteady, and in those days we did a lot of DJ and live instrument events in various Barcelona clubs and bars.

Chris told me that people always asked him how he was able to play guitar over vinyl, since the DJs are constantly changing the original pitch so that it is nowhere near 440 hz standard tuning. I had never thought about this because with the saxophone it's no problem, you can tune the instrument in one second, but a guitar has six strings to tune. Anyway Chris said something like »I find a way to do it. It's not a problem really. Bend the notes. Tune it a little bit.«

Barbican Centre, London, 2000

Out of Nowhere was a difficult album to make. I had lost touch with reality a little bit at that stage. To promote the album we played a special concert at the Barbican centre and once again I contacted my friend Anatole Kysk in Paris and requested more stage wear. Anatole had created the gorgeous blue sequined cape I wore for my horseback entrance at Sónar in '98, but at that time he ran his own wedding dress boutique.

I wanted two outfits for the show. One was supposed to be a bit like an underwater god and the other one was supposed to resemble the outfit of Ivan the Terrible in Eisenstein's classic movie. The underwater god headpiece was a copy of a headdress I had bought from a stage outfit vendor at the legendary Encantes flea market in Barcelona, which was originally worn in a stage show at the local Molino Varieté (a copy of the Moulin Rouge).

The show itself went well and paved my way to more shows with big orchestras like the Deutsche Opera orchestra (Berlin), Metropole Orchestra (Amsterdam) and Riga Symphony Orchestra. I'm still more comfortable working with jazz big bands though as they are naturally loud and the players are used to rhythm music.

Matti Knaapi and I had created a special instrument called photophone. It was played in a similar manner as a Theremin, but the way it functioned was totally different. I really love this curious instrument and go into more detail about it later in the book. The first song of the night was »Out of Nowhere«, a contemporary classical piece I had come up with in collaboration with Mike Kearsey. I play Photophone on that song and Matti thought it might be cool if we made a wireless version of the instrument so I could come on stage carrying it like a lantern. That worked out beautifully.

These pictures are by Antti Viitala.

Jimi Tenor And Rhythm Taxi, Berlin, 2004

Back in 2004, when Kabukabu were still called Rhythm Taxi, we decided to play a gig at Maria in Berlin. In a stroke of luck we could rehearse at the venue and get the sound exactly right. I stayed in the hotel next door and had my kids with me—it was a busy and stressful time in my life.

During the first rehearsal our guitarist Oghene Kologbo didn't show up and I was told he'd hurt himself playing football. He called me later and said he was sorry but he wouldn't be able to play. On the day of the show he came to rehearsal with his arm in a sling, and it all looked very legit, so we had to find another guitarist quickly! Timo Lassy said he knew a talented guy in Berlin called Kalle Kalima, and after a quick phone call he was in the band. He showed up an hour later and said that he'd already learned three of the songs on the drive to the venue! I was impressed, I don't think he played a wrong note all night and his soloing was excellent.

We had a stellar horn section for that show. There were the regular guys from my band, Timo Lassy, Jay Kortehisto and Jukka Eskola, and then Daniel Allen Oberto and Ben Abarbanell Wolff from Rhythm Taxi. We were on a two-week tour and had improvised a toga outfit for Jukka with a laurel of birch leaves, the Finnish midsummer night crown.

The gig was very exciting and we had so much energy and freedom on stage. When I listen back to the recordings it doesn't sound that tight, but to me live shows are like theatre; performance is about more than just playing the right notes. After the gig everyone was so loud backstage, shouting with exhilaration and relief. We made it! It was a new kind of experience for most of us, the band members were from literally all over the world and we had come together to make this show.

Still, I had a lot of stress that night. There are a lot of practical issues with a large group like that and also the money is tight when the band has 10 members. I was also travelling with my young kids and that created its own pressure. There were some really nice fans chatting to me backstage, but they didn't get the hint to disappear when the time came to count the money and pay the band. I ended up shouting at them until they left. If those people are reading this (I think they may not be my fans anymore!), I want to say that I'm sorry.

In 2003 I'd done a huge tour with the Jimi Tenor Big Band, playing 60 shows non-stop and it had been exhausting. On top of that, when I returned home from the tour and looked at the figures I realised that I'd lost 3000€. That was still fresh in my memory and returning to a bigger ensemble was a questionable move. Musically I would love to always play with a large band, but financially that is not possible.

World Expo, Shanghai, 2010

In 2010 I was in Shanghai playing at the World Expo as part of the Finnish envoy. I had toured in China a couple of years earlier and it was great to be back. My gig was in the bar district of Shanghai at a music club, which had no backstage so I had to change my outfit in a garage next door. The gig was great though and people were very enthusiastic about my performance. I love to play in small venues where it gets a bit rowdy and I can feel the audience near me. In bigger venues it's all a bit anonymous, especially if you're on tour and hang out mostly with your own people every day. My solo gigs are semi-improvised. I have a skeleton of the songs that I have pre-programmed so I usually play the start of the song quite normally and then start improvising. I compare my gigs to a TV chef on a cookery show. I have my ingredients on the table and with my skill I can turn them into something lovely.

Jori Hulkkonen was in Shanghai as well, DJing at the main Expo area for a large audience. We decided to go to the garment district together and visited this huge complex that's full of tailors. I asked for a pink suit and Jori ordered a suit that had one black trouser leg and one white, with the fabric reversed for the jacket so it looked a little like a chessboard. When we picked up the suits Jori was outraged. »What!? You've made me a suit that has one side black and one side white! I'm going to look like a chessboard!« It took the owner a little while to realise he was joking; I think something was lost in translation.

Ever since I'd seen this older, quite macho gentleman at the Barcelona city beach wearing a pink suit and smoking a cigar, I wanted to have my own pink suit. That guy even inspired me to buy some cigars, and you could get some nice Cuban cigars in Barcelona. My problem was that I have never smoked, so thought they tasted terrible and felt sick afterwards. I went to a menswear shop in downtown Barcelona where they had semi-tailored suits. Though they had some nice colours, they didn't have anything in pink so I ended up buying a sky blue suit from there.

In Shanghai we were in a hurry because we had to be at the airport in two days, but they told us the suits would be ready in a day and a half. They were also disconcertingly cheap, and we wondered how they could make them so fast. One guy in our group accidentally wandered downstairs looking for a toilet. He swears to god that he heard the sound of a whip and somebody screaming while the sewing machines were running non-stop! We were imagining a sweatshop full of kids down there. Obviously he could have imagined the whole thing though, who knows.

This photo was taken at a hotel in Switzerland when Nicole and I were playing a Cola & Jimmu show. I noticed the pink curtains and thought ›there's a picture‹.

Sauna, Lahti, 2006

In Winter 2006, I organised a snow-sculpting event in my hometown of Lahti. I had just moved back there from Barcelona and all sorts of vague childhood memories were returning to me. I was sure there'd been a snow sculpture event when I was younger so I decided to organise my own on the ice of lake Vesijärvi. I asked a relative who had a tractor to come and pile snow in small mounds, which we could then sculpt. It was harder work than I thought.

The high point of the event was when Seppo Renvall (standing in the back) erected his bubble sauna. Seppo is an artist who builds saunas out of stuff he finds at the location. Usually this is in an urban setting, so might be a big trash can for the swimming pool or a giant piece of plastic for the roof of the sauna. He usually finds bricks or stones so that the sauna retains its heat, and wood for the fire, though often he uses gas for practical reasons. It was −15 °C that day and it was fun to be in a sauna on the frozen lake. He put styrofoam on the ice to prevent it from melting and stop us getting frostbite.

Sauna is more than a way of life in Finland; it's actually like a religion. They can just as easily be used for a family event as a corporate meeting. Almost every home has a sauna attached and I think there are more saunas in Finland than people.

French Culture Centre, Nairobi, 2011

In around 2007, my brother moved to Kenya for a few years, and in 2011 I ended up playing a couple of concerts there, one in a French culture centre and the other in a game restaurant. Daniel Allen Oberto, the trumpet player in Kabukabu, had a project with local musicians in Nairobi, and I asked if I could join him as both an opportunity to see my brother and also visit Kenya for the first time.

    Nicole and I flew over there and there were plenty of rehearsals planned, but it turned out that most days were spent hanging around the practice room waiting for something to happen. The traffic in Nairobi is so chaotic that it's almost impossible for anyone to be on time. Usually cars were at a standstill on the roads, so on the day of the gig our driver suggested that we leave three hours early, even though the journey was only around thirty minutes on foot. I had my pink suit on and I was carrying my saxophone so they told me not to walk there. After two and a half hours in the car we were still nowhere near the venue so I decided to walk the rest of the journey with a Dutch cameraman who was travelling with us. There were no sidewalks but we walked in the gutter and made it to the venue very quickly. I was shocked by the traffic but I'm sure there are plenty of reasons why it's like that and I don't have a solution to fix it.

    We arrived on time and the gig at the French culture centre went smoothly. Before our performance they showed Mika Kaurismäki's *Mama Africa* documentary about Miriam Makeba. And by some kind of coincidence I later made music for Kati Juurus' documentary film *For Kibera!*, about the huge Kibera slum in Nairobi. I never went there myself but my brother visited several times because of his job. Kibera is world famous and popular for both tourists and NGOs looking to start a project.

    This photo was taken at a safari park just outside Nairobi. In my life I'd been on many photo safaris but this was my first time on a proper safari with real wild animals. The giraffe was standing right next to a picnic spot, which was surrounded by trees, bushes and grass—but no fences. There were plenty of lions in the park so we skipped the picnic!

objects

Flute

I was no child prodigy. I was interested in playing the flute, but at the conservatoire they told me that one must start with the piano. So I played piano even though I wasn't that good at it. Looking back, starting with piano made some kind of sense. The idea was that it's useful for understanding chord structures and to be honest I think it has helped me a lot as a music maker, so maybe the old folks at the conservatoire do know what they're doing.

When I was nine I got a chance to start playing the flute, not at the conservatoire, but at a workers' evening school. After a year or so, my teacher mentioned me to Tapio Jalas, who was a legendary teacher in Finland and the grandson of Jean Sibelius no less, and the following year I was studying flute with Jalas. For me this was wonderful. Jalas was a strict and enthusiastic teacher but unfortunately, I was a lazy student. He told my parents: »Jimi could be a great flautist but he only practices the easy bits«. It was a harsh critique, but entirely deserved and delivered with warmth and good intentions. I loved Jalas as a teacher and was devastated when he was kicked out of the conservatoire for having an affair with a student.

I guess I was a late bloomer in many ways. I was around twenty when I started to practice the sax properly. Maybe it was even later, I don't know. I have acquired most of my musical skills slowly as I went along. The 80s were a bad decade for flute in pop music and nobody was playing it. I was so happy in the 90s when flute became popular again; all thanks to hip hop samples!

I have an easy relationship with the flute. I always take it with me when I travel and it's fun to play in hotel rooms or even at airports. I got my basic technique from Tapio Jalas and I have created my own loose style of playing during the years. But my main interest has always been to make songs—to be a producer of records. In the conservatoire I was told that I couldn't start composition classes before doing the counterpoint. I was doing very well in music theory but was reluctant to start the counterpoint. In fact I didn't like the classical music style of writing the chords. For me the jazz style made much more sense, as the chord is what it is. Anyway when I was 16 I was listening to Finnish underground rock, Iggy Pop and Fela Kuti, and somehow the counterpoint didn't seem like the path to making that kind of music. I had typical teenager issues at that point. I just wanted to play in bands and thought classical music was shit. Playing in bands has always been great—the sense of excitement when you're in a really good band is totally unique, and for me the classical music world didn't offer anything like it.

Some years later in jazz school in Helsinki I heard music from Penderecki, Ligeti, Varese and Stravinsky and was also introduced to the ideas of John Cage. I had heard Steve Reich's music on TV and I was really interested in that. I love repetition. I also saw an exhibition of futurism around 1984 and I think that was the most influential event in my musical life up to that point. I saw images of Luigi Russolo posing with his noise machines and instantly wanted to make my own noise box as well!

I talked about the idea with my friends Matti Knaapi and Hannu »Enver« Mäkelä and Enver suggested we make the noise box using electricity and perhaps a magnetic tape. So Matti Knaapi ended up making that noise box. He used a bicycle dynamo for the energy source and the dynamo would give juice to a walkman. In the walkman there would be a cassette which could have any music on it. The faster you turned the dynamo the faster the tape would move. In practice the machine sounded something like when you scratch a record, but a bit more sinister perhaps. I was making an album with Edward Vesala in the late 90s and we used the noise box then. Edward told me about the sound that he heard when the pigs next door to his house (he lived in the countryside) were taken to the slaughterhouse. Edward demonstrated the crazy screaming ... I recorded that and used his scream in a lot of gigs later on via the noise box.

Korg MS20

A life-changing event happened to me in 1984. Someone told me about an auction house near my place in Helsinki where they sometimes have instruments for sale. Since most people who go to the auctions look for gold and antiques, they aren't that interested in musical instruments. I went there and sure enough there was this special looking synthesizer, a Korg MS20. I put in a bid and got it for 450FMK, which is about 80€.

You can hear the MS20 on every one of my albums. I have used it for noise effects on soundtracks, as a wah-wah effect for my flute; I have triggered it with drums and of course used it as a regular synth as well. On my *Sähkömies* album I used it a lot for bass.

My MS 20 is now very battered. I have tortured it on stage over the years, doing all kinds of Jimi Hendrix style theatrical moves. Luckily I never decided to try and set it on fire because that would probably have been the end of it.

So many people ask to take photos of my MS20. I was playing a festival gig with Tony Allen and the French band Air were playing after us on the same stage. They also use MS20 and had a special roadie to adjust the sounds ready for the next song during the gig. They saw my MS20 and they couldn't believe it. They loved it and asked to take photos of it.

At some point I got frustrated about the missing keys. I decided to make extensions to the battered keys out of veneer. I have plenty of veneer that I use for making wooden flutes. I glued them on the keys and it worked really well, for a while, and then they started to get loose one by one. At the moment I have fixed the keys with pieces of plexiglass and white silicone. None of them have come out yet, so I'm good.

I used the MS20 on »Take Me Baby«. The honking backbeat sound is a sample I made with the MS20. I sampled it on a Roland digital delay pedal and triggered the sound with Roland 606 drum machine. I re-used the liberated MS20 for the soft reverb soaked backbeat sound that wanders throughout the track every two bars, randomly going up and down.

On my 50th birthday I made a special cake shaped like my MS20. It looked great and it also tasted good!

Sirkka The Drum Machine

When I was working with the Shamans we often played industrial gigs. At the time I was obsessed with the futurists and the idea of noise as music. When we arrived at one gig in Turku the promoter suggested we go to the junkyard and fetch some barrels to bang them during the gig. We hit them with metal sticks and pummelled them with hammer drills and the noise they made was different to everything else we had on stage. No drum or cymbal sounds so cold and hard while still retaining a little tonality. So we decided to use barrels at all our shows. Thanks to the guy in Turku! For one TV appearance we even designed a special holder for the hammer drills to be used with the barrels.

For another TV performance Matti Knaapi and I decided to build a huge drum machine, something that would look amazing. The machine we ended up building looked a bit like a windmill, and though it was big and looked great, it didn't sound that good. It was very difficult to make something that looked cool, kept good time and still sounded right.

So we decided to build a new electro-mechanical drum machine that would actually sound good. Matti had found a computer model of a champagne bottling device, which had an interesting jerky movement. We thought that by changing the direction of the movement we could make that machine hit an object very hard without slowing itself down. We attached a strong spring to the piston so that a lead weight would jump out, strike the sound source (in this case a barrel) and then recoil in an instant. It sounded amazing! Not only was it very hard hitting but it didn't slow down at all, thanks in part to the washing machine motor we used to power it. On top of all that, Sirkka also worked as a drum stand for the barrels, and was collapsible. It could be dismantled into three parts for transportation. We took it on one tour in Germany, but some of the welding came loose in the bad roads of Poland. On that tour Sirkka didn't keep time so well, but it still looked impressive!

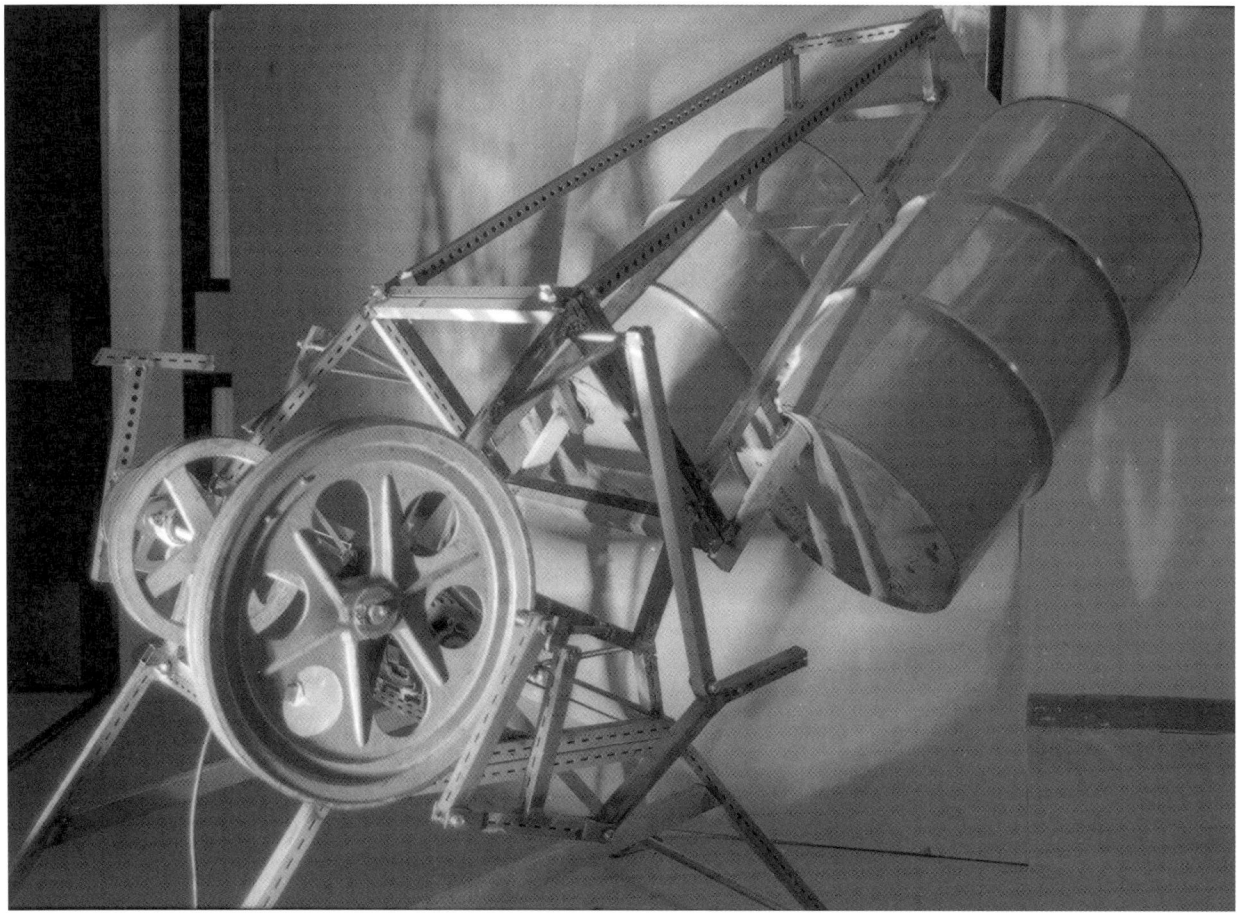

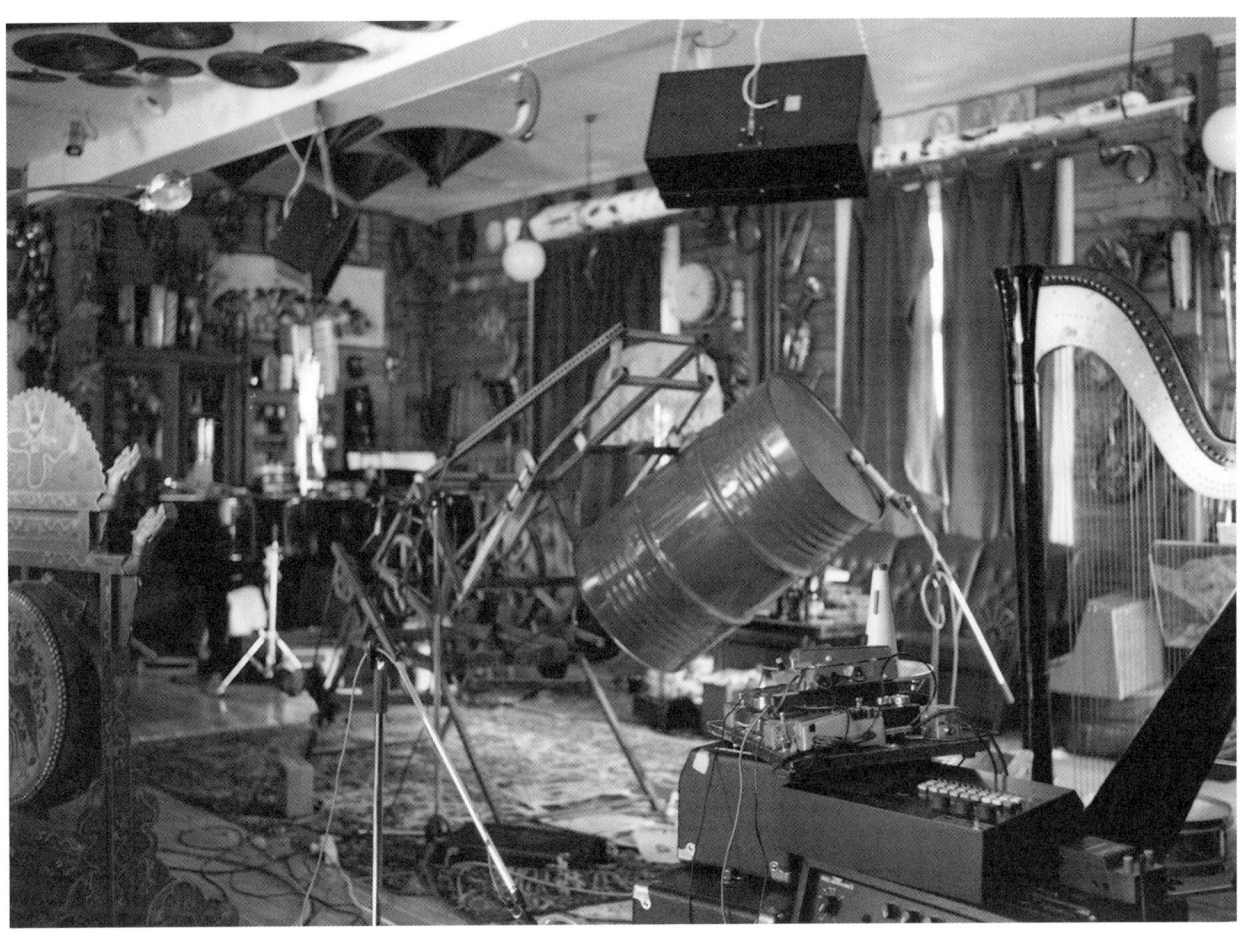

We played a lot of gigs in the Soviet Union back then and Sirkka was with us for all of them until one fateful performance in Riga. After the gig the local crew dismantled it, but did their job a little too well. We were taking a regular bus back to Tallinn and the drum machine had to be stored in pieces in the aisles. Sadly we could never put it back together again. You can hear this machine on a track called 380v by Jimi Tenor and his Shamans.

Atari 520

This is from Kauklahti, during my stay at the communist party dancehall. The rest of the building was an icebox but my studio was happening. You can see my Korg Polysix and MS-20, Ritm-2 and Roland 606. In interviews I used to say that I didn't use computers, but one UK magazine caught me because of this photo! There's an Atari 520 monitor lurking over my shoulder. It's true I used that Atari on a couple of tracks on the *Europa* album. Those songs were a bit more complicated and my qy10 ran out of memory. I had no choice, honest! I'm not anti-computer really, at least nowadays, but composing on software doesn't suit the way I work. If I sit in front of a computer trying to write I'll quickly give up, but if I have a real instrument or synth the ideas start to flow freely. I think I find it easier to work with a tool in my hands, whether it's an instrument or a camera. You can see here that my microphone stand is a photo stand. I use photo stands for everything.

Around this time our cat went up a huge birch tree next to the house and got stuck up there over night. I called the firemen, but they were on strike and couldn't come. Then the cat went even higher and there was really no way anyone could climb up there. Two days later I called the firemen in desperation. I was crying and the firemen were very sorry, but they still couldn't come. In the end my friend Timo Rauhala said one of the people he gives golf lessons to ran a phone company and they have cranes. Quite soon a crane came to our yard and I went up to the tree in the crane cabin. The cat grabbed me very hard up there and held on tight all the way down, then promptly ran off to wee.

Log-O-Phone

I'm originally from Lahti in Finland. When I was growing up, Lahti was a furniture and woodworking town and the famous ball chair by Eero Aarnio was manufactured there. Quite soon after our kids were born we moved there from Barcelona, which was a big change mentally.

    I'd been thinking about making more instruments for a while and since we were in Lahti I thought it made sense to sign up to a woodworking class and learn how to make wooden flutes. Initially I started by making just the head joint out of wood then using plastic for the rest of the flute. I wanted to make an alto flute and I found this bent white plastic tube, which enabled me to reach further with my little finger. I also made one pad out of an old tenor sax pad. I was very happy with this flute. It had a pentatonic scale and the root note was A flat.

At this point I became obsessed with wooden flutes and woodwork in general. I started to question why Finland doesn't have a strong percussion tradition? We have plenty of wood and some of it is perfect for percussion instruments. Ash for instance, which is used in guitars like the Telecaster, resonates very well. At some point I said kind of jokingly that the only rhythm I heard when I was a kid was my dad chopping logs with his axe. So I thought I would make an instrument called the ›log-o-phone‹.

It's like a marimba with logs as the reeds that you hit. My ›log-o-phone‹ was made out of ash that had fallen on the road by our summerhouse and sounded fantastic! I had read that Pat Patrick from Sun Ra's band had made bass marimbas and I had actually heard them in one of the Sun Ra albums ... perhaps *Cosmic Equation*. So at the woodworking class I started to make reeds for a bass marimba out of the leftover wood that I had. I used sewage pipes as resonators and it sounded great!

My marimba wasn't in any particular tuning. I just wanted it to sound great and perhaps give me ideas for compositions. I didn't want to know if it had any scale. As a matter of fact, I use a lot of primitive instruments to start a composition. Most of the time the tuning of these instruments doesn't fit the standard 440 hz tuning, which I find wonderful. The problems arise when one tries to play these songs live with a band and realizes that the song is not in any discernible key! This is also the best thing about this approach as you end up using different keys to bring a composition to life. It's refreshing to use unusual keys and I think it gives an extra dimension to an album.

Zither

When we first moved to Barcelona I converted our garage into a studio, and though the walls were a bit too hard for good acoustics, it was just about passable. Around that same time I heard Sun Ra's »I Am An Instrument«, which was recorded by my friend Paul Smith. Paul went to Philadelphia in order to make a spoken word album with Sun Ra and »I Am An Instrument« was the closest thing to a spoken word track that Sun Ra gave him. Sun Ra played zither on that track, so when I saw one at the flea market in Portugal I bought it. Thankfully it easily fit in my suitcase and survived the journey home intact.

    I loved that instrument. I would tune it in totally random scales and use it as inspiration for writing. This was the same approach I used later with my log-o-phone. Some of the thinner strings on the zither made a cool twangy sound which I found really unique. I have used it a lot for special effects and even as a reverb unit.

    When I moved my studio back into my apartment, I needed to downsize because even with the storage space and linen closet, there was not enough room for everything. I can't live my life like Lary 7! I decided that since I'd had plenty of use out of the zither it should go back to the flea market and re-incarnate. I hope it ended up in someone else's recording studio and not as a decoration in a music pub.

Photophone

Somewhere along the line Matti Knaapi and I made a special instrument for DJs called *Liberace*. It was a 12" iron disk with holes drilled in it and the idea was to put it on a Technics turntable. On top of the iron LP there was a controller that had seven keys. Each key was connected to a Fender Rhodes pick-up and these pick-ups were lined up to the series of holes that had been drilled in the disc. The idea was that the holes were drilled to make a musical scale and one could play bass notes with this controller.

  Well, *Liberace* may have worked but it was very difficult to use. The original idea for the instrument came from the Hammond organ and I thought that perhaps we could use the same idea, but with optical sound instead of magnetic. The result was the photophone. We made a film where sound waves were exposed to create a chromatic scale. This film would spin in a household fan. A light source shone through the film and I collected the sounds with an optical sensor from the air. It is played a little bit like a Theremin, but it works in a completely different way.

  The photophone is easy to play and makes a very easily distinguishable high pitch sound. The sound is not a continuous square wave like on a Theremin or synth, but sounds like it's made out of small pieces—a bit like a football referee's whistle. You can hear it on *Out of Nowhere*, »Nuclear Fusion« (*Higher Planes*) and »Hot Baby« (*Joystone*).

  In a strange way the photophone is a sampler. We have tried to expose samples on the rotating disk as well, but the resolution is just not high enough. Anyway the photophone disk spins so fast that the longest sample it could hold would be far too short for any practical use.

MOGADISHU

Score For Night In Mogadishu Ave

This is the way my scores used to look for the Kabukabu songs. I didn't normally write down much for bass, guitar or drums, the player would need to listen to my demos and figure out their parts from there. So these scores are really just for structure and for horns. In this kind of music the horns normally need to play together as a section, so their parts need to be written down to some extent.

The second page is my saxophone and flute part. At some point I started to write more with notation programs. I prefer to write with pencil and paper, but for practical reasons the computer crept into my work. A lot of musicians say that music sounds better if it has been written down by hand rather than with a computer and there might be something in that. At least I find it much easier to read handwritten sheet music. The spacing is better and it looks more personal.

I started keeping most of my sheet music on a server in around 2003, well before anyone was talking about the cloud! It was practical when we did our Jimi Tenor big band tour that year. Especially since sheet music easily gets lost and fans like to take them from the stage as souvenirs. These days I've replaced the server with a folder in my Google drive. As for the physical papers, well they're all over the place. Most of them are long gone or totally unorganised in random drawers.

I belong to the school of composers that try to make the parts as enjoyable for the players as possible. What I mean by that is that my music isn't absolute music. I normally know the players that will play the parts and I try to write for their abilities. Of course sometimes one must push the envelope a little bit—my music doesn't look that technical, but in fact it's not that easy to play.

Solo Gig Settings

Over the years I have made hundreds of this type of setting sheet, one for every single gig where I use electronics. The first time I used them was perhaps when Khan of Finland and I played a gig at El Sensorium in Brooklyn in 1993. Or perhaps it was a year later when we went on the Sähkö-tour in the U.K. and Ilpo Väisänen suggested we make this kind of reference. Either way, it's been a good system.

I like to work with hands-on equipment. Typically this means that there is no memory for any settings in the device. But that's the way I like it. I know my synths and drum machines very well and it only takes me seconds to adjust the settings for a next song.

These papers are a bit like shorthand. You only write the essential information about the settings. All the rest is trivial and you just need to know it. Sometimes I write the first word for each verse or the starting note of the saxophone line. This can be really helpful if you experience a temporary blackout on stage. I get very easily distracted and start to play all over the place if I see something special in the audience. Even if I just see people getting excited I still get carried away. As a result I normally play with my eyes shut. I quite often wander away from the microphone when I play sax because I can't see where it is. I don't care though ... it's part of the show!

This particular reference sheet was for a gig at Café Oto in London. There are settings for a modular system and an MFB synth. There are also some sequencer settings and drum pattern numbers.

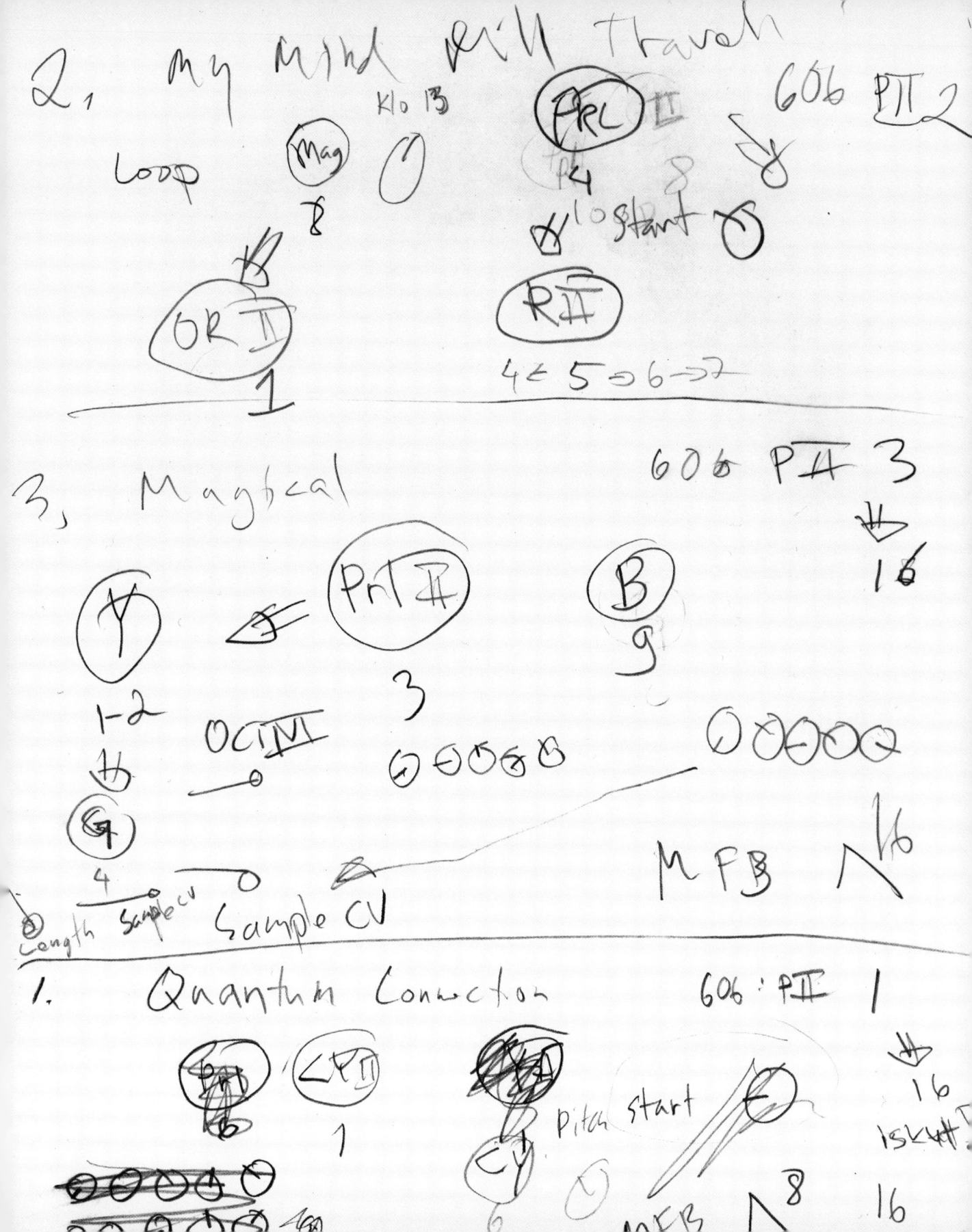

Kimono

I bought this wedding kimono in Nagoya, Japan in 2008. It's very heavy and very fancy, but it was actually super cheap. Apparently people don't want a second hand wedding kimono no matter how nice it is. This particular kimono has gold and silver embroidered images of storks and bamboo leaves and is very beautiful. I have a special room in my house where I keep some of my stage outfits from the past. Many aren't in great condition anymore because stage life ruins clothes, so this kimono is one of the most beautiful things in the room.

Every once in a while I take my 140-year-old camera out of the closet and take a portrait with it. It's a 13 cm × 18 cm large format camera and for this picture I used it with a Schneider lens from the 60s and a flash. I shot it directly onto photo paper to get the orthochromatic look. The model is my partner Toimi Tytti. and Ilpo Väisänen said that Tytti looks like a Russian Spy in this picture!

It was a long walk to that kimono shop in Nagoya because I had hurt myself the previous week while ski jumping in Lahti. I come from a ski jumping town and I had done it a lot when I was a kid. But by this time I was 40 years old and obviously my reaction time wasn't quite what it used to be. My body mustn't have been as resilient as when I was younger either, since I broke my collarbone and badly bruised my hip. I had to take a taxi back from the kimono shop because I couldn't walk anymore. So there was no more ski jumping for me after that. The hip still hurts every once in a while ...

Jimi By Thron Ullberg, New York City, 1992

I moved to New York in 1992. My girlfriend Tiina Huckowski had moved there so I followed suit. I had just been staying in Berlin for 6 months, where I made one album for the Finnish label Bad Vugum.

I was 27, but still didn't know what to do with my life. I thought my music career had failed or at least there was no way to make a living out of it; making industrial music using scrap metal was fun, but a financial challenge. So I tried to become a photographer—after all I'd been doing photography all my life, why couldn't it work out as a career. I enrolled in this art school in uptown Manhattan where I took some lighting courses, a film developing course and a nude model photography course. At the school I met Thron Ullberg (who ended up taking the cover photo for *Intervision*) and we went for a little photo safari at the waterfront in Williamsburg. In those days that area was in ruins. Someone said the mafia owned it and had big plans for property development. There were some abandoned buildings there and we took some photos inside. I'd bought a really cool ice cream cone suit from a legendary second hand warehouse called Domsey's and I wanted to pose in that outfit.

For a long time I had been obsessed with the idea of 3-D photography and especially the green-red aspect about it. I had many pairs of the green-red glasses, including a special pair I'd fashioned from welder's safety-goggles, which I used to wear when I went dancing at the techno clubs in Finland.

For this picture I had a special idea. What if we put a red filter in front of the camera lens and then we put a green filter in front of a powerful flash. Hopefully in the foreground the flash filter and the camera filter would sort of cancel each other out so that the lighting would be fairly neutral in colour. But everything in the background would be red, since the power of the flash wouldn't reach so far. I think it turned out quite well! The glasses are racquetball glasses I had bought in a dime store.

Washington Heights Rooftop Portrait, New York City, 1992

When I first arrived in New York we stayed at our friend Lada Ferrari's house on 176th Street, near Broadway. I've always liked to explore the areas where I live for photo-shoots and in Washington Heights there were a lot of interesting places. I like wastelands, overgrown parks and abandoned buildings. Bridges are beautiful and normally there are no other people there, just cars passing by, but since they can't stop everyone remains totally anonymous. One day Tiina and I went on a photo safari to Washington Bridge and found loads of small hubcaps on the way. I made necklaces out of them—the Jaguar one was especially pretty. New York is a great place for good junk. It also has a great rooftop culture and I loved to go up there for photos. This photo was taken on the roof of the building on 176th Street and you can see Washington Bridge in the background.

I fell in love with New York. It was a fun place to be. I loved all the Latin music and culture, the bars and food. A couple of times I walked up to Washington Heights from downtown in the evening. It's a long walk. I loved the area between 110th street and 165th street, strolling past people playing dominos or drinking beer. In New York you can experience the city in myriad of different ways, and if you get into trouble you're in at the deep end. I got mugged a couple of times and it's not fun! And then there are the super rich people ... well I didn't have any contact with them really. At least knowingly that is. Perhaps I brushed shoulders with them at the art openings, which I did go to quite a bit. Free drinks you know!

Opening At Orensanz Foundation, New York City, 1993

The first couple of years in New York we moved around every few months, heading from Washington Heights to Red Hook and then Williamsburg. I've always been a suburb guy and have practically never lived in the centre of any city. Life's much more interesting in the outskirts of town. The people there are more real in a way, there are no tourists and it's way cheaper to live.

The first place we settled properly was in an apartment in Williamsburg. At the time it was a fairly rough place. We lived on the corner of South 2nd Street and Bedford Ave. South 2nd was a party street for people from DR and Puerto Rico and the noise from the cars and different PA systems was overwhelming. On top of that we lived next to the fire department and without exception there were sirens going off every night. Needless to say that in NY the sirens are loud! The good thing about this was that we could make as much noise as we wanted in our home recording studio, which was especially handy as my friend Can (Khan of Finland) had moved in with us.

But at that point I thought my future would be in photography. I had been doing Jimi Tenor and his Shamans for years and although we had a lot of fun it seemed like a dead end. I felt that for my personality industrial noise in the long term was a bit much. Also I wanted to experience the world and keeping a group together at the same time seemed like an impossible task.

I tried to get assistant work in professional photo studios. Scandinavian assistants have a good reputation in New York. Again, with my personality it wasn't easy to get any of those jobs. I'm too quiet and I think social skills are the most important ones when you're an assistant.

I kept taking art photos though and started to print huge images on car bonnets and any scrap metal I could find. I discovered a special liquid emulsion that you could spread on any surface. I could paint the emulsion on car hoods and then sponge on the developer and fixer. Naturally all this would have to be done in darkness or in red light so I used to transform our bedroom into a darkroom. After a while our apartment was full of my car hoods and all kinds of large pictures. I had crazy energy back then, I just wanted to do stuff and New York is a perfect place for that. My only problem was the lack of money, and that was a major problem.

Our landlord was the brother of Angel Orensanz, the famous Spanish sculptor. I think he was happy to have us as lodgers because we were artsy types, but we were behind on the rent for most of the year we lived there. Mr. Orensanz would often call round for a coffee and even showed us the best Caribbean snack bar in Brooklyn at the M-train stop. It sold alcapurrias and crispy pork skin. I love that kind of food! He was a good landlord and wanted to help with our money troubles. He suggested that we could clean this old synagogue they had bought at Norfolk St. in East Village in exchange for one month's rent. When Mr. Orensanz came to collect the next month's rent he noticed my photos in the living room and offered to host an exhibition at their synagogue as they had plans to convert it into an art gallery.

So on May 28th 1993 I had an opening there. I managed to get Finlandia vodka from the Finnish consulate and it ended up being quite a happening! Tiina and I performed at the dais of the temple. I was playing a modified vacuum cleaner, which I turned into a sort of strange trombone. Instead of sucking I converted the cleaner to blow instead. I connected a rubber glove finger in the airflow to act like the »lips« of the trombone and I placed an aluminium light reflector as the bell for a loud sound. Tiina had been doing dance performances at the El Sensorium underground club events and her style was a modified Butoh. The performance went down very well, perhaps better than the photos! I guess deep down I knew I was more of a performer than a photographer, but at that point I had nothing going on in music and it looked like a permanent state of affairs. I didn't even have a saxophone mouthpiece any more.

Empire State Building Reflexion, New York City, 1993

Though Mr. Orensanz was a pleasant and patient landlord, the apartment on South 2nd did have its drawbacks. It was a top floor apartment with broken heating and a leaking roof and it was getting a bit too wild because of crack, violence and noise. So for multiple reasons we wanted to find a better apartment, and luckily I managed to find a job to pay for it.

My friend Hitoshi Toyoda was working at the photo booth on the 86th floor of the Empire State Building and told me about a job vacancy. One of the staff called Amy had quit and they were desperate to find someone new. I went up there to the observation level and gave a very unconvincing performance in the job interview. It required good selling skills, and that's never been my forte. The photography in the booth was high quality but the settings were always the same so it didn't really require any photographic skills. I only got the job because I was ready to start the same day.

The job was taking photos of tourists in front of three different backdrops: The Statue of Liberty, King Kong and the Empire State Building. People would sit in front of the backdrop and we would take a photo with this huge 8×10" camera—the same size that Avedon used in his famous shots. The photo quality was exceptional, but the tourists didn't care, for them it was just a silly picture with King Kong.

We had to sell the idea of the picture to the tourists. Sometimes we would ask the first customers to pose for free so that others would notice how much fun it actually was. Then most of the time after the first shots people would queue non-stop to have their picture taken. It was a bit of fun and a good photo to show the folks back home. There's a picture by Hitoshi Toyoda in which I try to »hypnotise« a customer to take the photo. I think I'm waving a pendulum in front of her.

This job was very good for me. I could pay my rent easily, save the deposit to move apartments and also buy some music equipment. This equipment was crucial in making *Sähkömies*. I bought an Oberheim DX drum machine, which at that time was almost the cheapest drum machine you could get. I loved it! A Japanese guy in a Soho music store used to work for Roland and he burned me a couple of extra chips for the DX. They were kick, snare and hi-hat sounds from a Roland 909. They sounded great, a funny combination of 909 and DX. I used those drum sounds on »Take Me Baby« for example. I still use the DX now and it's always on my studio desk hooked up and ready to go. But if you're doing anything that is dreamy or romantic … that is not your drum machine!

The job at the Empire State Building was nice in many other ways too. I was normally on the night shift and in the evenings it was beautiful up there. When we had breaks it was fun to go and look at the views. I worked there on New Year's Eve and I was looking forward to the fireworks. I thought I would be immersed in multi-coloured light but it turned out that the fireworks were 300 meters below us and I barely saw them at all! But at midnight the city looked like it was bathing in a blue haze. At first I was wondering what it was, and then I realised it was people taking flash photos. From that

sort of distance the flash looks blue and at midnight everybody was taking a picture! The blue haze only lasted for about one or two minutes.

    I was taking photography lessons in a photo school uptown around that time as well. They suggested buying a couple of photo stands, a good tripod, a light meter and some flashes. I still have every one of these pieces of equipment and I use them weekly. Whenever I need extra microphone stands I use these photo stands. They have the same thread as microphones so it's very convenient. This is my advice to anybody who wants to be in music and is also interested in video and photography: get a photo stand! You won't regret it.

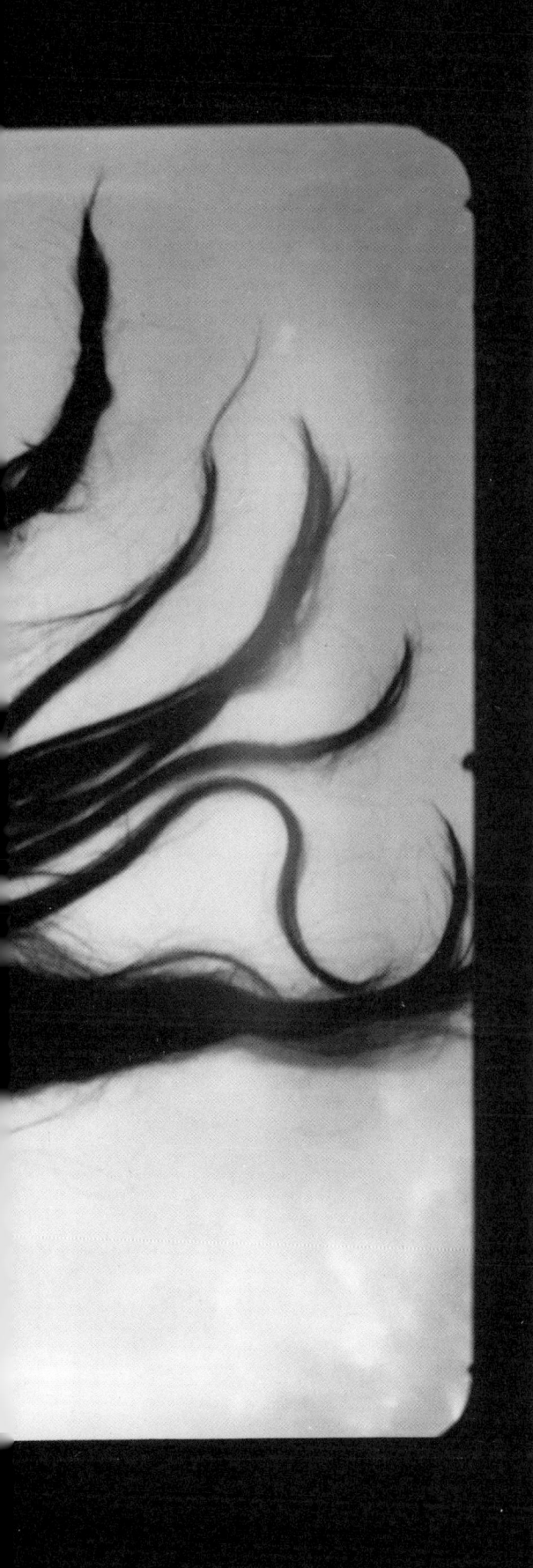

Tiina Medusa, New York City, 1993

Tiina had a crazy amount of special clothes and it was very convenient for me to use them in PR photos. She was kind of my stylist at the time and I knew we were doing good stuff. Tiina wasn't that familiar with cameras, but we would set up the camera together and she actually took really good pictures. I have a similar attitude to photo shoots as recording sessions. Studio surroundings don't excite me that much. I prefer to record music at home and also to take pictures where I live. I like to work fast and enjoy sketch-like results.

    I used to go to Coney Island a lot in the early 90s. I like beaches during winter and I love abandoned amusement parks. Another reason to go to Coney Island was the flea markets. You could get some really cool stuff. I bought a BMX there once and rode it all the way back to Williamsburg.

    One day at the flea market I saw a beautiful Land Polaroid camera. It wasn't automatic like the new cameras but had manual exposure and a flash shoe so you could use it with studio flash. You couldn't get film for that camera anymore so I converted it into a 9×12 cm sheet film camera. I had dreamed about a 9×12 cm camera and this was it! It was very professional and had a great lens and a distance meter.

    This photo of Tiina as Medusa was taken with that Polaroid. Tiina had a lot of hair, so it looked nice. These are the customised welding glasses I wore to the raves in Finland. I'd put Lee filters on the lenses—one eye was red and the other was green. I used the glasses to read 3-D comics as well, but in the clubs it was totally amazing. The green and red made everything look a bit more 3-D than real life. It was uncanny, and when you took them off after the party your left eye would see everything in green and your right eye in red for quite some time—the opposite colours to the goggles.

    Unfortunately I am terrible with nice things and have a habit of losing stuff. So in 1994 when we moved to Finland I lost the Land Polaroid camera. I also lost the Ricoh camera that I used for most of the Z Factor shots.

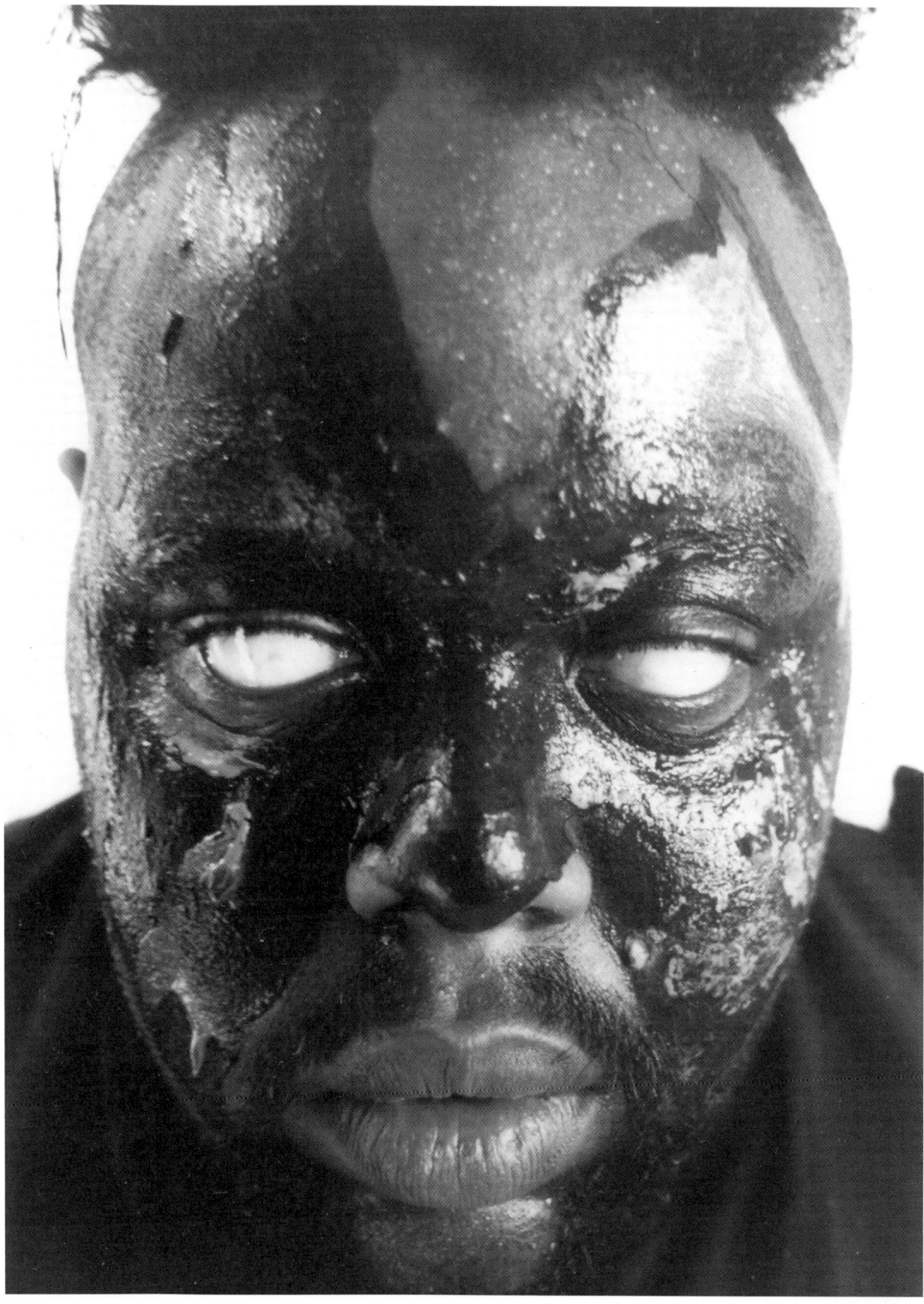

Wrestlers Grand St. Gym, Williamsburg, New York City, 1993

There was a group of Argentinian artists who ran an underground club in Williamsburg called El Sensorium and after a while I became a regular performer at their events. Can Oral and I played an electronic music set in an inflatable balloon. These balloons were a regular piece by one of the artists at El Sensorium. Once I organised a photo shoot there with the »fat lady« I had made friends with at the Coney Island sideshow. These events were great happenings. Gradually the group became more and more well known and expanded their events to clubs in Manhattan as well. I guess I fell out with the main guy Mariano at this point, which was too bad because these events were fantastic.

Outside of El Sensorium there were no club events in Williamsburg because everybody said it was too dangerous. Crack cocaine had become really popular in '93 and our corner was a distribution point. The sidewalks were covered with the tiny plastic tubes with different coloured tops. The last flight of stairs from our flat to the roof was full of kids taking crack in the evenings. It wasn't too pleasant but we left them alone and they did the same. Still, this was one of the reasons we eventually moved out of the South 2nd apartment.

Once we were invited to a one off club night in Williamsburg. I was on the guest list and was on my way there when I heard the event was stopped because there was a shoot out. I think some people died there and feel very fortunate that I didn't arrive sooner. It must sound strange that Williamsburg was like this in the early 90s but it was very rough in those days. Then quite soon after I left it became seriously gentrified. I get it because it's just one stop from Manhattan on the L train. I met a film cameraman called Alejandro Serrano at the El Sensorium events and became good friends with him. He would later shoot my documentary film »Sähkö-The Movie«. He told me about this catch wrestling gym at Grand St. in Williamsburg. Catch wrestling is not a big thing in NYC. I think at that point there were only two gyms in the whole city that had a scene. So we went to see the show at Grand St. and took our cameras along. I think we had a Polaroid or something. The evening was great! I loved everything about it, I'm a circus fan and this reminded me a lot of the circus.

In Mexican wrestling all the performers have their own special character. They dress up like some sort of super heroes with a lot of masks and make up. El Expectro had a quite classic luchador outfit with his mask, cape and high wrestling boots. His speciality was to throw his opponent out into the audience and then jump over the ropes swan style and land on them. But none of the wrestlers were professional; it was a community event really. We went backstage after the show and suggested taking some photos of them in my studio.

Z Factor, New York City, 1993–1994

In Finland I'd seen a photo book by Joel-Peter Witkin. I was fascinated by his photography and I was hoping to do something that was staged with special looking characters as models. I also liked the way he scratched the negatives.

At that time I was buying used comics from the street vendors. I like the imagery and thought that if I could find interesting models I could transform them into some sort of superheroes. I cut single frames from the comics and tried to recreate them, making the costumes out of the great junk I found on my photo safaris.

I placed an ad in Village Voice—»Looking for unusual looking models for art photos«—and was brought in for an interview at the paper. They didn't want any dodgy perverts or porn photographers placing ads in their respectable publication. They were sure that I was going to shoot porn rather than art photos. Either that or perhaps sexually harass wanna-be models. Well, I told them explicitly that it was not my intention to harass the models and only had interest in fine art.

I got more than ten replies for my ad and went to meet every single one of them. A couple of the applicants definitely wanted only sexual harassment, no photos needed! One of these guys was »Dave«. That's the name he gave me anyway. He wanted to be bound and masked and most importantly have his penis tied up. I wasn't so impressed by him and wanted him to get out of our house. I was pretty rude but that just seemed to excite him even more. Eventually we managed to get rid of him but he kept calling and wanted to do more sessions sans camera, offering to pay us 50$. I got inspiration from Dave to do my song ›Sugardaddy‹.

Most of the people who called me because of the ad were actually not that unusual looking at all. They were just people who wanted to get one more shot for their portfolio. I managed to get more interesting looking people from other sources. I loved NYC because people were into doing stuff. I've always been a doer. I'm excited about projects and I want to get them done. Sure it's expensive to live in New York and people need money. That's definitely one reason people have drive, but people also do neighbourhood projects, volunteer, put on special club nights etc. all without any pay.

Adam (previous page). As I said at South 2nd street we shared our flat with Can »Khan of Finland« Oral, whom I'd originally met in Finland. He'd been in the country to visit his mum, saw a poster for a Jimi Tenor and His Shamans show and came to the gig. I visited Can later on in Frankfurt to make some music and hang out, then again called him from NY and suggested he move there with us.

Adam was a friend of Can's that lived in Chelsea Hotel. The Hotel had two sides: one for daily guests like a regular hotel, and one for permanent guests who would pay monthly. Adam used to visit our place regularly and one day I asked him to pose in one of my pictures. The characters in the comic books seem to glow quite often, so I painted Adam's body with silver paint. I used the cool hubcaps I had found at Washington Bridge for the outfit as well as some electric relays from the street as his belt.

Bobby (right page). Tiina knew a dwarf called Bobby and thought he would make a good model for my photos. The comic book character I had in mind for him had four hands. So we decided that Tiina would wear a totally black outfit and we would shoot against a black backdrop. She wouldn't be seen, but her hands would be visible as Bobby's extra hands.

Bobby was involved in the »legalize marijuana« movement. I think he was quite high up in the organisation, but I can't be sure. He told us about the plan to drive around the US and throw marijuana seeds everywhere. That way there would simply be too many plants to get rid of. He also took ketamine and missed our first photo-shoot because he was too high. I called him but couldn't understand any words other than ketamine. Well, he showed up the next time and was very professional.

Following pages:

Doll Woman. I met her when I was studying photography uptown in the fancy photo school uptown. She was one of the models on my nude photography course. She was a fun person so I asked her to come and pose for a photo at my studio. We had just moved to Union Avenue and I had enough space there for a backdrop.

I kept going to Canal Street Plastics and some other outlets in that area where they sold all kinds of stuff from bankruptcies. I found a box of plastic dolls and hung them from fishing lines in my studio.

El Expectro. I'd been completely won over by El Expectro at the catch-wrestling event in Williamsburg. He had the coolest outfit and the most highflying moves. I think they were all taking big risks because they were amateurs and I'm not sure how much they practiced. El Expectro showed up to the shoot with a bodyguard. I have a feeling their experience in the neighbourhood was markedly different to ours. Anyway the bodyguard was nervous. I used hot lights (no flash) and I must have used too many because all of a sudden the fuses went off. It was evening and was very dark in the room. I saw the bodyguard reaching for his coat pocket and thought »oh no, he's going to shoot«, but El Expetro had figured out we were just some artsy kids and told the other guy »tranquillo«. I quickly went next door to get power from our neighbours so we could carry on with the photo shoot.

Hisao. A lot of my friends in New York were from Japan. I met Hisao at some party and we made friends instantly. Hisao was a professional photographer and specialised in taking pictures of objects. He worked in a photo studio and sometimes we could go there to take my promo pictures. My first album for Sähkö was just about to come out and I thought it would be great to have real professional promo shots. But I had still had ambitions in photography and I asked if I could take a picture of Hisao for my Z-Factor collection. He had a unique style and I thought it could be great. I wanted to show his brains in the picture so we went and bought some lamb brains, which we had to cook so that they would stay firm for the photo. I wanted to do a double exposure in the camera. Hisao had a Mamiya 645 that had a Polaroid back. We used the Polaroid 55 that gives both positive and negative, as I wanted to make big prints of the photo later on. It was really hard to place the images together with a perfect angle but in the end we got it right. Hisao ended up doing a lot of photography for me, including the *Europ*a album cover and plenty of PR shots and live pictures.

Following pages:

Finnegan. A friend of mine knew I was taking this series of photos and he said he knew a guy who was very skinny. He'd been run over by a truck or something so had been lay down for a long time and lost a lot of weight and muscle. Also this guy Finnegan had a special look, a bit like the punk rock style. So I went to see him at his house on the Lower East Side. He was very nice and we agreed to do some photos.

His comic book character was chained to some crazy weights. I used the larger hubcaps I'd found for this purpose. And again I went to the famous Industrial Plastics at Canal Street and bought some Fresnel lenses that I hung in the air with fishing lines. At that time I also made some slapstick Super 8 movies with Jusu Lounela. Finnegan had a small role in one called »The Wrestling Man 2«.

Jamie. I met plenty of creative people via Finnegan. This image of Jamie is actually the first one in my series. I bought a super wide-angle lens to get the exaggerated superhero looks. He wore some strange fly-man outfit. Since this photo worked so well I thought the whole project would be easy. Jamie was into comics and he understood the concept immediately, I think that helped a lot.

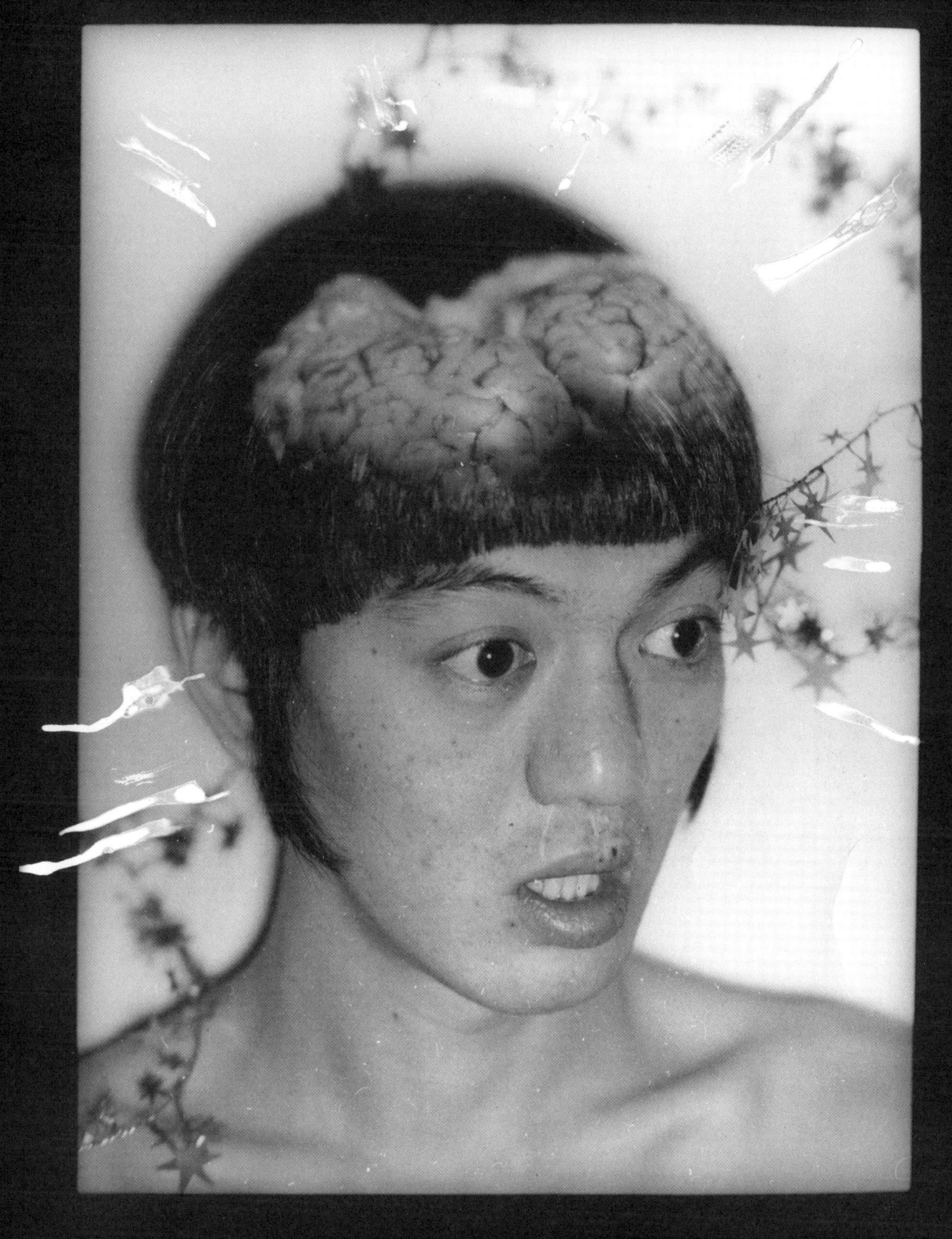

Kenya. I think this image was based on Mr. Fantastic from the Fantastic Four. I used another of those hubcap things that I had found to make the round symbol from the chest of the original comic book character. Then I painted the 60s looking disc in the back. I thought the whole set looked very 60s. Kenya's fiancée was out of shot holding the other end of the fishing lines, which were helping her keep the pose. They were very sweet people and later asked me to take photos of their wedding. That wedding photography experience was so difficult that these days I respect wedding photographers a lot. I am far too shy for that job.

Following pages:

Lada and Pia. Lada was one of my closest friends in NY. When we first arrived there Tiina and I stayed at her place in Washington Heights. Lada and Pia both worked as dancers in erotic clubs. In fact a lot of my female friends were doing it. It was quick money with few questions asked.

I had seen transparent plastic shoes in a Helmut Newton book and thought they were incredible. I managed to get two pairs in a dime store. Then I fashioned the metal bras out of single use aluminium pots. The arm shields are made from some sort of gym equipment.

Otter. I'd made music for a film called Odd Globular Beings. The director Markku Nordstrom was a friend of Otter, who was a legendary character in the East Village. She had a performance piece where she cut her arm with a knife to draw a glassful of blood, and then drank the blood. She'd lost her front teeth in a car accident and had them replaced with permanent vampire teeth. She was a magnetic character and looked gorgeous in the rubber cat suit. For the close up I used a slide projector to get that stage spotlight look.

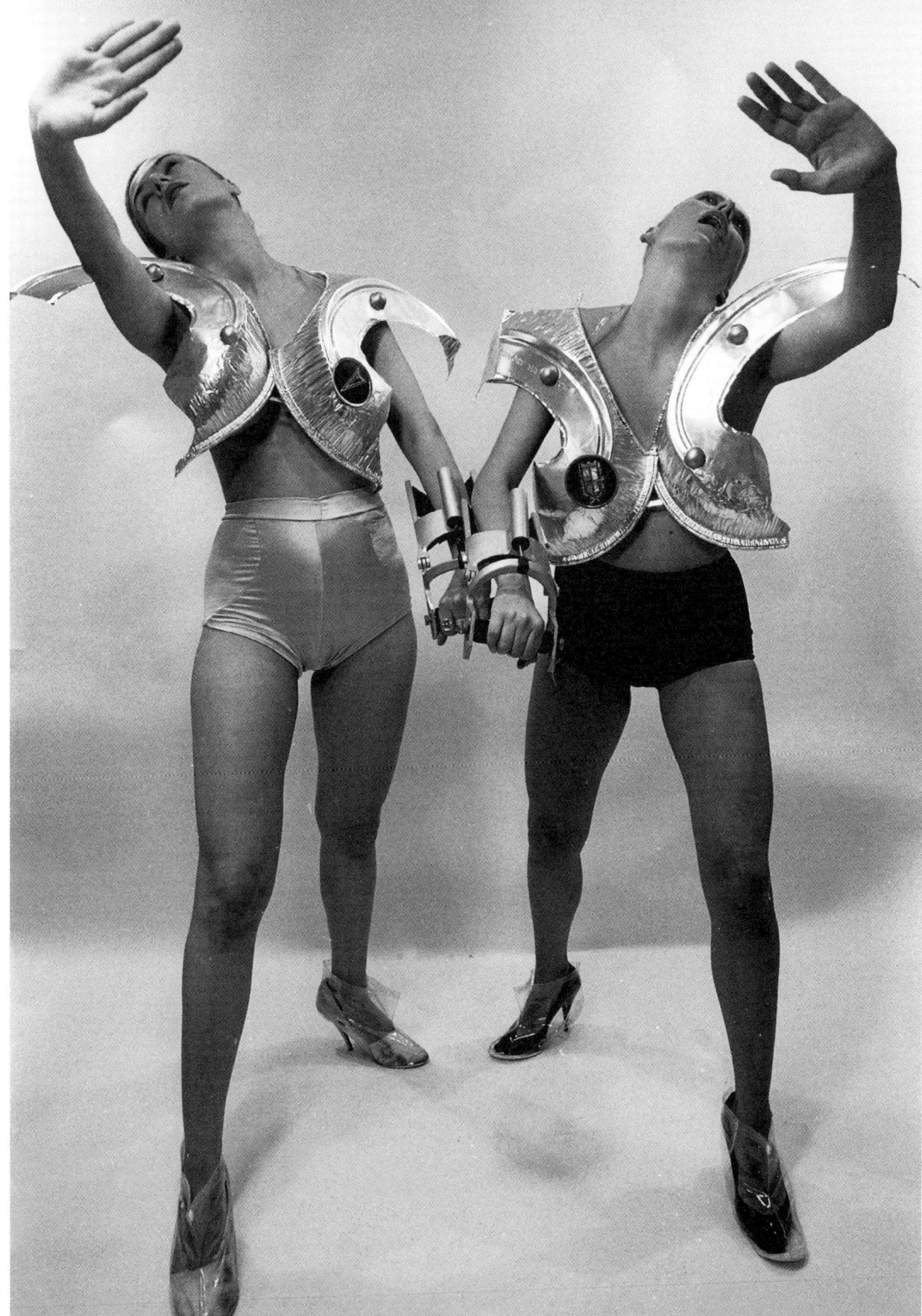

Tacheles Exhibition, Berlin, 1994

I lived in Berlin for six months before I moved to New York. At some stage my friend Rotta-Pete (rat-Pete—he had a pet rat) got in touch and suggested that I should show my work in Tacheles. Pete always knew the latest galleries and cultural happenings in Berlin. Since this was before emails it was quite difficult to organise the exhibition from New York. Tacheles didn't have much of a budget at all and for a while my pictures were stuck in customs because no one could afford to pay the fees. In the end I think we managed to explain to customs that these images really had no value and were kind of trash—I guess they took a look and struggled to disagree ...

I had to guard the show so I made recordings in the gallery. Ilpo also helped me to build the show and he too made a set up in the gallery. He played at the opening too. During the exhibition I bought an EKO Rimini organ from a man who lived in a Berlin suburb. I loved that organ and immediately made the track »Fantom (the wandering ghost)« with it. The recording was actually done in the gallery during the exhibition with the set up in this picture plus the EKO organ. For the nerds: that is a Digi Tech GSP5 guitar effect rack module. I used it for reverb. I would normally put a little bit of distortion on the reverb too. That's a great unit.

Tacheles had no heating and it was winter. Luckily my Italian ex-flatmates from Kreuzberg worked in a deli across the road. The deli had heating and more importantly good red wine. I would sneak out from the exhibition every once in a while to go there. I didn't think it was likely that someone would run away with my car bonnet pieces.

Urinator, New York City, 1994

While I was in New York my friend Jusu Lounela and I made some 8 mm and 16 mm trash films. This is a still from »Urinator«, our movie about a super villain who holds the world hostage with his pee. Why did we do it? We had way too much energy and needed an outlet. And I guess we took inspiration from John Waters and wanted to do something tasteless and funny. Everything about the film was trashy and camp. We've shown it at some garbage film festivals but I don't think many people liked it. I have to agree with them! But we did get the great Japanese punk band Ultra Bidé to play the opening titles, so something good came out of it. Anyway at that time in New York most people didn't question what you were doing so much. »Oh, a camp film about a guy waving dildos and peeing everywhere … count me in!«

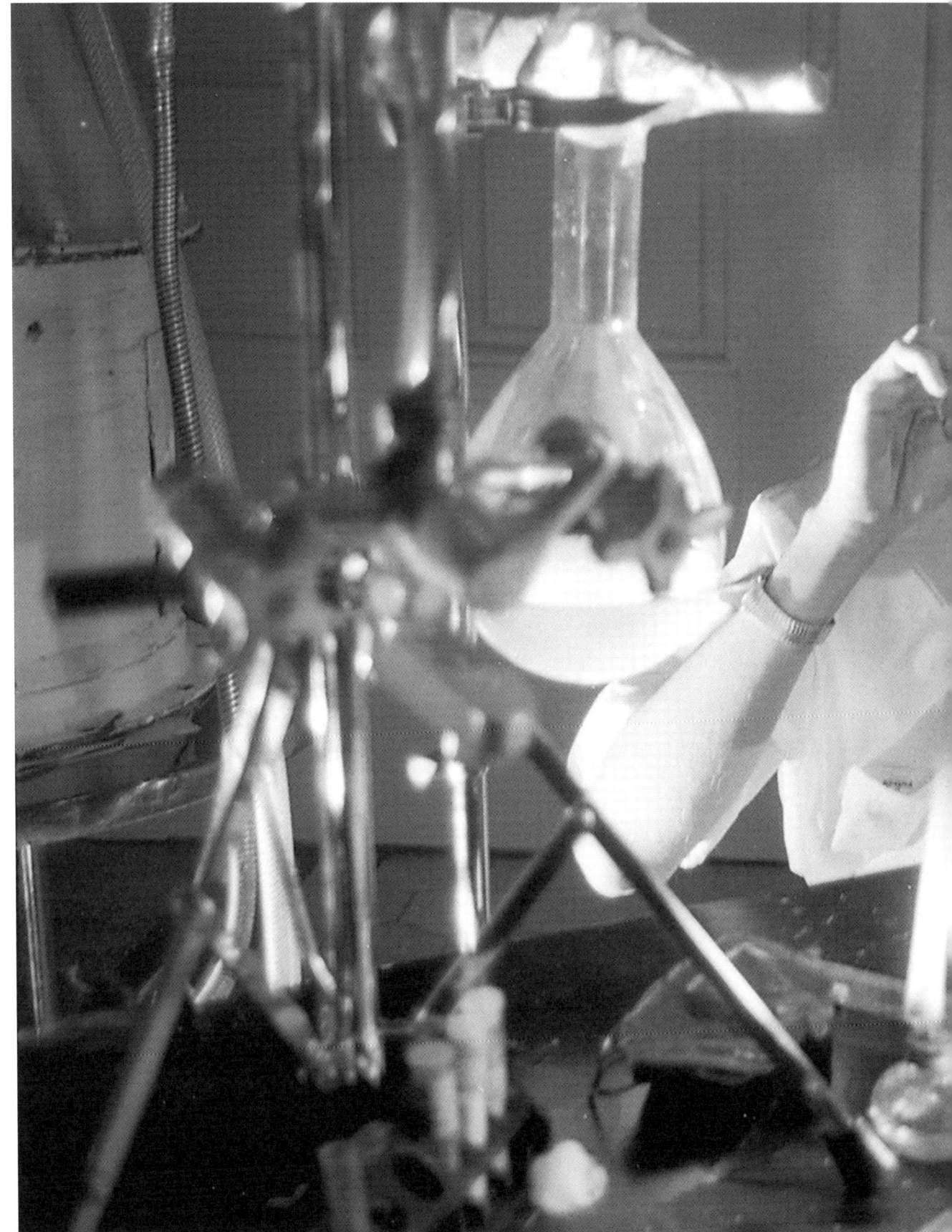

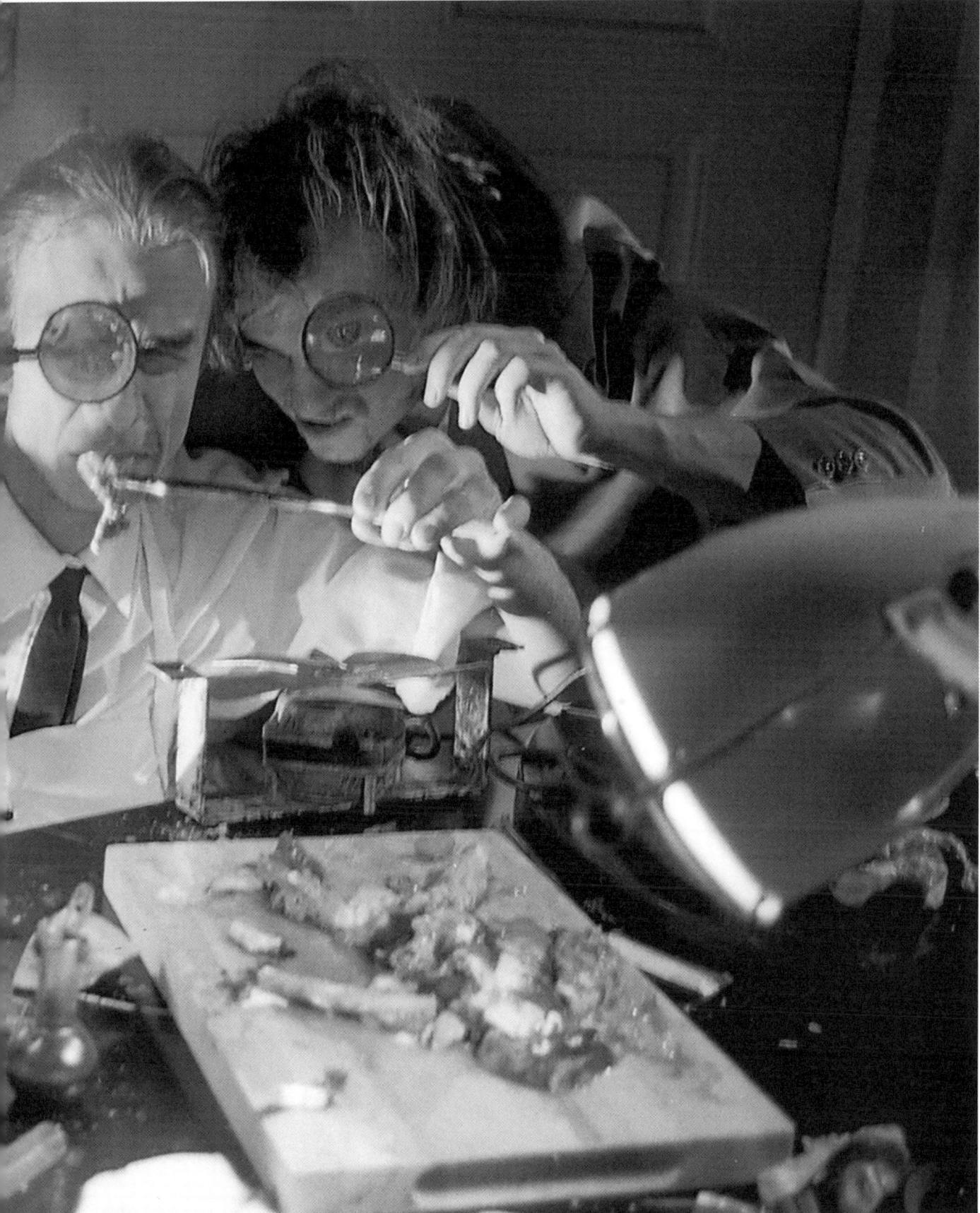

Midsummer Night Video, Lake Päijänne, 1998

Almost all Finnish summerhouses are by a lake, and ours is in the south of Finland by lake Päijänne. There are quite often beautiful foggy mornings there. I wanted to do a video for »Midsummer Night«, which would include some Finnish midsummer-magic—a mermaid seen diving and stuff.

    Predictably there was no morning fog on the day of the shoot but we made a good video anyway. My dad borrowed a nice wooden rowing boat from a neighbour and my girlfriend Tiina was the woman diving.

    I'd picked up that beautiful EKO Rimini organ in Berlin for 50 Deutschmarks when I was doing my exhibition in Tacheles. I used it on every album after that, but when we needed an organ to appear from the lake, the EKO had to go for a swim. If you visit the lake hoping to find the organ, you'll be out of luck—we rescued it from the water but sadly it never worked again. I've donated many of my old instruments to video shoots over the years.

Autobahn, Finland, 2011

One day when I was driving home from the studio I saw a dead badger on the road. It occurred to me that I had never seen a live badger. It's a shame that we see dead animals on the road every day and don't really think anything about it. After that, I started to get out of my car whenever I saw roadkill and have a look at it. Strangely, many times they looked like ready-made abstract paintings. So I started taking pictures of them with my 13×18 cm negative size camera. I always took the pictures directly from above in order that they would have no perspective, but look like paintings.

    In fact, when I was on the safari in Kenya, I only took two photos. The first was of the giraffe which features earlier in the book, and the second was of a dead dog on the side of the road. I asked the safari guide to pull over so I could get out and document it and he must have thought I was crazy.

    These are sad pictures and I wish there was a way to stop roadkill. Maybe traffic could be a bit slower. When I was taking these pictures on motorways and roads I noticed how overwhelmingly loud cars and trucks are. The noise itself would make an animal crossing the road dizzy. I had to stop this project because it was too dangerous for me and I think it's quite illegal as well.

outro

Coney Island, New York, 2010

I can't remember the first time I went to Coney Island but I have a feeling it was during the wintertime. It quickly became one of my favourite places. I love amusement parks in general but have a special affection for old, run down amusement parks. There was one in Barcelona on Montjuïc, which was really trashy and unpopular. I loved it. There was a haunted house and the guys who ran it would wear ghost costumes and surprise you in the dark rooms. But Coney Island is much more than just an amusement park. It has a huge history, but most of that is just a memory now. It's surrounded by the huge Trump (senior) buildings, which are quite rough these days.

There were many excellent flea markets on Coney Island. Khan of Finland bought a great tube guitar amp from there. The asking prize was 100$. Khan laughed and said 1$! In the end he bought it with 10$. There was a nice camera shop there as well with several Kiev 80' in the window. I bought my fancy Land Polaroid from that shop. When I did my Z-factor series, I went to the Coney Island sideshow to look for models.

When you walk towards Brighton Beach there are racquetball courts, Ukranians playing chess and lots of Russian and Ukranian restaurants. We used to go to those restaurants all the time in the early 90s. The area is called »Little Odessa« and there was almost a Soviet atmosphere inside. There would be a dance band playing Russian songs, pickled watermelons and cabbage. I love Russian and Ukranian food.

Pickles are one of my obsessions. While I'm writing this I have Japanese asazuke-pickles getting ready on the table. My grandmother would make huge jars of Finnish style pickled gherkins and my brother and I would eat them like candy. I heard that one could buy individually vacuum packed pickles in the supermarket in New York in the 70s. And kids would eat them like it was a candy—a great idea!

Whenever I go to a new town I try to find the local pickles. In New York it's all about Essex Street Pickles, but in Tokyo I go the pickle street at Monzen Nakacho that leads to a temple. There's a restaurant there called Kintame that serves a pickle lunch, three servings of different pickles and one bowl of rice. It's so simple but perhaps the most memorable lunch of my life!

That's it folks! Time to go and squeeze the liquid out of my asazuke!

Photo credits

Abdissa Assefa: page 60, 63
Antti Viitala: page 57, 92, 93, 94, 95
David Pugh: page 49
Hisao Oka: page 172
Hitoshi Toyoda: page 149, 151, 153, 174, 175
Ilkka Mattila: page 25, 64, 65
Jimi Tenor: page 12, 21, 25, 36, 37, 41, 46, 53, 58, 60, 61, 62, 68, 69, 85, 87, 101, 105, 108, 111, 112, 116, 122, 124, 125, 130, 139, 154, 156, 157, 159, 161, 162, 163, 165, 166, 167, 169, 170, 171, 176, 178, 182, 185, 189, backcover
Jimi Tenor Archive: page 18, 30, 31, 65, 83, 103
Jochen Ströh: page 66, 67
Joel Hietanen: page 131
Jouko Lehtola: page 75, 79, 114, 118, 120, 121
Julian Leitenstorfer: page 132
Lada Ferrari: page 149
Lary 7: page 33, 34, 35, 50
Marjaana Turpeinen: page 72, 73
Matti Knaapi: page 117
Ragnheiður Pálsdóttir: page 183
Raija Lehto: page 127
Risto Roman: page 184
Russell Haswell: page 51
Sökö Kaukoranta: page 180
Sonar Festival: page 88
Thomas Ecke: page 96, 98, 99
Thron Ullberg: page 8, 17, 20, 142, 144
Tiina Huczkowski: page 1, 20, 22, 24, 25, 146, 179
Tommi Grönlund: cover, page 26, 27, 28, 37, 38, 54, 55, 58, 71, 80, 84, 85, 90, 102, 103, 128

© Ventil Verlag UG (haftungsbeschränkt) & Co. KG, Mainz, 2022
Use of this material, in full or in part, is only permitted
with expressly agreement of the publisher. All rights reserved.

In Cooperation
with Tapete Records

1st edition, May 2022
ISBN 978-3-95575-174-6

Editorial team: Gunther Buskies, Daniel Jahn, Patrick Ryder
Design & layout: Oliver Schmitt
Print & binding: Maincontor

Ventil Verlag, Boppstr. 25, D-55118 Mainz
www.ventil-verlag.de

Jimi Tenor – NY / HEL / BARCA

Jimi Tenor – Deep Sound Learning (1993–2000)

Jimi Tenor – Multiversum